GLENCOE

PHYSICS

Principles and Problems

Physics Lab and Pocket Lab Worksheets

 **Glencoe McGraw-Hill**

New York, New York   Columbus, Ohio   Woodland Hills, California   Peoria, Illinois

GLENCOE
PHYSICS
Principles and Problems

Student Edition

Teacher Wraparound Edition

Teacher Classroom Resources

Transparency Package with Transparency Masters

Laboratory Manual SE and TE

Physics Lab and Pocket Lab Worksheets

Study Guide SE and TE

Chapter Assessment

Tech Prep Applications

Critical Thinking

Reteaching

Enrichment

Physics Skills

Supplemental Problems

Problems and Solutions Manual

Spanish Resources

Lesson Plans with block scheduling

Technology

TestCheck Software (Win/Mac)

MindJogger Videoquizzes

Interactive Lesson Planner

Interactive Teacher Edition

Website at *science.glencoe.com*

Physics for the Computer Age CD-ROM (Win/Mac)

The Glencoe Science Professional Development Series

Graphing Calculators in the Science Classroom

Cooperative Learning in the Science Classroom

Alternate Assessment in the Science Classroom

Performance Assessment in the Science Classroom

Lab and Safety Skills in the Science Classroom

Glencoe/McGraw-Hill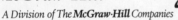

A Division of The McGraw-Hill Companies

Send all inquiries to:
Glencoe/McGraw-Hill
8787 Orion Place
Columbus, Ohio 43240

ISBN 0-07-825937-1
Printed in the United States of America.

1 2 3 4 5 6 7 8 9 024 07 06 05 04 03 02 01

Contents

Contents *continued*

To the Teacher

Physics Lab and Pocket Lab Worksheets contains expanded versions of the Physics Labs and Pocket Labs featured in the Student Edition of *Physics: Principles and Problems.* All written material is repeated so that students will be able to read and complete an activity without the need for a textbook on the lab table. The worksheets also include expanded data tables and write-on lines so that students can record data, calculations, answers, and conclusions directly on the sheets. The worksheets are not only a convenient management tool for you but also help students stay on task as they work through the labs.

Safety Symbols

In *Physics Lab and Pocket Lab Worksheets*, you will find several safety symbols that alert you to possible hazards and dangers in a laboratory activity. Be sure that you understand the meaning of each symbol before you begin an experiment. Take necessary precautions to avoid injury to yourself and others and to prevent damage to school property.

	DISPOSAL ALERT This symbol appears when care must be taken to dispose of materials properly.		**SKIN PROTECTION SAFETY** This symbol appears when use of caustic chemicals might irritate the skin or when contact with microorganisms might transmit infection.
	BIOLOGICAL HAZARD This symbol appears when there is danger involving bacteria, fungi, or protists.		**CLOTHING PROTECTION SAFETY** This symbol appears when substances used could stain or burn clothing.
	OPEN FLAME ALERT This symbol appears when use of an open flame could cause a fire or an explosion.		**FIRE SAFETY** This symbol appears when care should be taken around open flames.
	THERMAL SAFETY This symbol appears as a reminder to use caution when handling hot objects.		**EXPLOSION SAFETY** This symbol appears when the misuse of chemicals could cause an explosion.
	SHARP OBJECT SAFETY This symbol appears when a danger of cuts or punctures caused by the use of sharp objects exists.		**EYE SAFETY** This symbol appears when a danger to the eyes exists. Safety goggles should be worn when this symbol appears.
	FUME SAFETY This symbol appears when chemicals or chemical reactions could cause dangerous fumes.		**POISON SAFETY** This symbol appears when poisonous substances are used.
	ELECTRICAL SAFETY This symbol appears when care should be taken when using electrical equipment.		**CHEMICAL SAFETY** This symbol appears when chemicals used can cause burns or are poisonous if absorbed through the skin.

Physics Lab Equipment List

Quantity needed for one lab group

Description	Amount	Lab number
alligator clips	4	24
ammeter, 0-50 mA	1	22, 31
apron	1	12
balance, pan or electronic	1	1, 2, 13
ball, plastic foam	1	20
beaker, 250 mL	1	12, 13
bedsheet	1/class	28
blindfold	1	28
blocks, wood	4	4, 5, 9
car, battery powered	1	4, 5, 26
cardboard or corkboard, 21 cm × 28 cm	1	8
cart, lab	1	9, 11
cart, lab, with spring	1	9
cell, solar	1	31
channel, grooved (U-channel or shelf bracket)	1	27
clamps, C	2	9
clay, 2 small balls	1	16, 18, 19, 21, 26
coil, iron or air-core solenoid	1	24
compass, magnetic	1	24
cup, plastic	1	20
diffraction grating	1	19
egg, raw	1	1
electrical leads	4	24, 31
film canister, 35 mm with lid	1	13
film canister, 35 mm with resistor	3	22
fishing line	3 m	28
floor tile, rectangular piece	3	2
floor tile, triangular piece	1	2
goggles, 1 pair per student	2	12, 15, 22, 28
graduated cylinder, 1000 mL	1	15
graphite, bottle of liquid	1	20
hot plate (or Bunsen burner)	1	12

Description	Amount	Lab number
index cards, unlined, 4 inch × 6 inch	5	16, 19
lamps, miniature with socket	3	23, 24
Light Emitting Diode (LED), bicolor	1	29
Light Emitting Diode (LED), green	1	29
Light Emitting Diode (LED), red	1	29
lens, concave	1	18
lens, convex	1	18
lightbulb, 40-W filament in fixture	1	16, 19
magnet, disc	1	25
magnet, permanent bar	2	26
marble, glass	1	26
mass, 1 kg	1	6, 11
mass, .05 kg	1	9, 11
meterstick	1	3, 4, 6, 9, 10, 11, 14, 19
mirror, flat (approx. 10 cm × 15 cm)	6	16
multimeter	1	22
nail, medium	1	16
nail, small	1	18
paper, graph	1	2, 5, 17, 26, 30
paper, white	2	8, 18, 21
paper, 1 m × 10 m	1	4
paper clips	2	25
pen, colored marking	6	27
pen, marking	1	3, 17
pencil	1	8
pennies	25	13, 20, 30
pie pan, 9-inch aluminum	6	20, 28
plastic dish, semicircular	1	17
plastic drop cloth, 3 m × 3 m	1	1

Description	Amount	Lab number
polystyrene block, 30 cm × 30 cm	1	20
power supply, 0–12 VDC	1	22, 23, 24, 29
protractor	1	4
pushpins	2	8
ramp (board) 0.5–1.0 m	1	11
resistor, 470 Ω	1	24, 29
ring stand with crossbar and clamp	1	24, 25
ruler, 30 cm	2	2, 8, 16, 17, 18, 21, 31
ruler, grooved	1	26
scale, 20-N spring	1	6, 9
scale, 250-g spring	1	13
softball	1	7
spring, coil (Slinky type)	1	14
steel ball, 3 mm	12	21
steel ball, 6 mm	1	26
steel ball, 2 cm	2	27
steel ball, 1 inch	1	5
stoppers, # 0 rubber	36/class	28
stopwatch	1	3, 4, 5, 6, 7, 9, 10, 11, 12, 14
straw, drinking	1	20

Description	Amount	Lab number
string, 30 cm	1	8
string, 10 m	1	3
tape, masking	10 cm	3, 4, 5, 6, 9, 11, 19, 25, 26
tape measure	1	15
tape, transparent	30 cm	1, 20, 21
thermometer, 0–150°C	1	12, 15
thread	105 cm	8, 20, 24
track, grooved	90 cm	5
tray, cafeteria	1	26
tube, hollow glass, 40-cm length	1	15
tuning fork	1	15
tuning fork hammer	1	15
voltmeter, 0–5 VDC	1	29, 31
wave tank	1	26
wire, connecting	6	22, 23, 29
wire, electrical 5–30 cm	4	2
wire, enameled coils	2	25
wire, iron, 20-cm lengths of thick insulated	2	24
wood, 1.5 meter 1 × 2	4	28
wool, piece	1	20

Pocket Lab Equipment List

Quantity needed for one lab group

Description	Amount	Pocket Lab number
ammeter	1	22-2, 22-4, 23-1, 23-2, 23-3, 25-2, 25-3, 29-1
aquarium	1	18-6
audio amplifier, mini	1	26-2, 26-3
ball	2	7-4
ball, 0.1-kg	1	7-1
ball, 0.2-kg	1	7-1
ball, rubber	1	3-1
ball, steel	2	5-1, 5-2
ball, steel, 12-mm	1	28-1

Description	Amount	Pocket Lab number
ball, steel, 1-in.	1	6-1
ball, steel, 3-mm	2	24-2
ball, steel, 6-mm	1	26-1
ball, steel, 9-mm	1	25-4
balloon	1	20-1, 20-2
balls, steel, assorted mass	3	11-2
battery, D cell	1	22-1
beaker, 1000-mL	1	17-2
beaker, 100-mL	1	12-2, 27-1
beaker, 250-mL	2	12-2, 12-3, 13-2

Description	Amount	Pocket Lab number		Description	Amount	Pocket Lab number
book	1	5-1, 5-2		lamp and socket, miniature	1	25-2
bowling ball	1	5-3		lamp with dimmer	1	16-2, 27-2
camera	1	18-1		laser pointer	1	17-3
cardboard, 10 cm × 30 cm	1	6-3		laser, He-Ne	1	19-2, 28-3
cart, laboratory	2	5-4, 6-5, 9-1		LED, red	1	29-2
cart, laboratory, spring loaded	1	11-2		lens, converging	1	18-6, 18-7
cellophane, red and blue	1	19-3		level, bubble	1	5-4
circular object	4	2-2		lightbulb socket	1	17-3, 19-1
clay	100 g	8-1, 18-3, 18-7, 26-1		lightbulb, 100-W	1	17-3
cloth, wool	1	20-1, 20-2, 21-1		lightbulb, 100-W, clear	1	19-1
cloud chamber	1	30-2		lightbulb, small	1	18-7
coffee filter	5	6-4		lightbulbs, three different	3	16-1
coiled spring toy	1	14-2		magnet	1	26-1
coin, dime	1	15-2		magnet, disk	2	24-1, 24-2, 31-1
coin, nickel	1	15-2		magnet, neodymium	2	25-1, 25-4, 30-2
coin, penny	5	1-1, 15-2		magnets, assorted shapes	several	24-3
coin, quarter	3	11-1, 15-2		marble, glass	4	28-1
cup, foam	2	12-1		marble, steel	4	28-1
cup, paper	1	8-3		mass, 0.05-kg	2	6-5
diffraction grating	1	16-2, 19-1, 27-2, 28-2, 28-3		mass, 0.1-kg	2	6-5
				mass, 0.2-kg	2	6-5
				mass, 0.5-kg	1	6-3, 10-3
dropper	1	12-3		mass, 1.0-kg	1	6-3, 8-2, 10-1, 10-2
dry ice	2 lb	30-2				
electroscope	1	20-1, 20-2		meterstick	1	2-1, 2-2, 4-1, 5-1, 5-2, 6-4, 11-2, 15-1
ethanol, 95%, denatured	30 mL	30-2				
eyeglasses	several pairs	18-5				
filter, blue	1	27-1		miniature lamp	1	22-1
filter, green	1	27-1		miniature lamp and socket	2	22-2
filter, polarizing	1	16-4		miniplug	2	26-3
filter, red	1	16-3, 27-1		mirror	1	17-3
flashlight	1	27-1		mirror, concave	1	18-2, 18-3
fluorescein	10 g	27-1		mirror, convex	1	18-3
food coloring	2 mL	8-3, 12-3		mirror, makeup	1	18-4
frequency generator	1	15-1		mirror, plane	1	18-1
galvanometer	1	25-1		motor, DC, miniature	1	25-3
Geiger counter	1	30-1		movie screen	1	19-2
generator, DC	1	25-2		musical instrument	several	15-1
gloves	1	12-2		nail, medium	1	24-3
golf ball	1	7-2, 17-2		needle	1	13-2
hose, garden	1	17-4		nut, hexagonal	1	17-2
household appliances	several	22-3		paper	3 m	3-1
ice cubes	2	12-1		paper clip	1	13-2
jumping disk	1	13-3		paper, graph	3	2-2, 3-1, 16-1

Description	Amount	Pocket Lab number	Description	Amount	Pocket Lab number
paper, white	6	1-1, 13-1, 24-1, 24-2, 28-3, 30-1	string	10 m	2-1, 2-2, 5-4, 6-2, 6-5, 7-3, 8-1, 8-2, 10-1, 10-2, 10-3, 24-3
paper, tracing	1	3-2			
pencil	1	8-3			
pen, felt-tipped	1	3-2	support rod	1	10-3
pie pan, aluminum, 9 inch	1	28-1	table	1	7-1
pith ball	1	21-1	tape player or radio	1	26-3
plastic disk	2	31-1	tape recorder	1	3-1, 15-1
plastic foam, 30 cm × 30 cm	1	21-1	tape recorder tape	1	3-1
power supply, DC, variable 0–15 V	1	22-2, 18-7, 22-4, 23-1, 23-2, 23-3, 24-3, 25-3, 29-1, 29-2	tape, masking	1.5 m	5-1, 5-4, 8-1, 22-4, 24-3
			tape, transparent	20 cm	1-1, 11-1, 30-1
power supply, spectrum tube	1	28-2	telephone	1	31-2
projection wave tank	1	14-1, 14-3	telephone pick-up coil	1	26-2
radiation source, needle mounted, alpha	1	30-2	tennis ball	1	17-1
			thermistor	1	29-1
razor blade, steel	1	13-2	thermometer	2	12-1, 12-2, 22-4
resistor, 10-Ω 1%	1	23-3			
resistor, 470-Ω	1	29-2	thread, nylon	20 cm	21-1
resistor, assorted values	several	22-4	tubing, copper, 1 m × 1/2-in. diameter	1	25-4
resistor, same value	4	23-1, 23-2			
rope	5 m	9-2	TV monitor	1	3-2
rubber cement	1 mL	31-1	U-channel	1	5-1, 5-2
ruler	1	11-1, 17-2	Variac (variable AC power supply)	1	19-1
ruler, grooved	1	26-1, 28-1			
ruler, metric	1	13-1	video camcorder	1	3-2
skateboard	2	9-2	voltmeter	1	23-3, 25-3
soap bubble wand	1	16-3	wheel-and-axle system	1	10-3
soap solution	10 mL	16-3	wire	10 cm	22-1
solenoid	1	24-3, 25-1	wire leads with alligator clips	6	22-4, 23-1, 23-2, 23-3, 25-3, 26-3, 29-1
solenoid, air core	2	26-3			
spectrum tube	2	28-2			
spring scale, 10-N	2	6-2, 9-1			
spring scale, 20-N	1	8-2, 10-1, 10-2	wire screen, window, 10 cm × 10 cm	1	19-2
staple	1	13-2	wire, #26 or #28	1 m	25-1
stopper, rubber, one-hole	1	7-3			
stopwatch	3	5-1, 5-3, 6-1, 6-4, 7-2, 9-1, 12-2, 14-1, 25-4			
straw, plastic, drinking	1	8-1, 21-1			

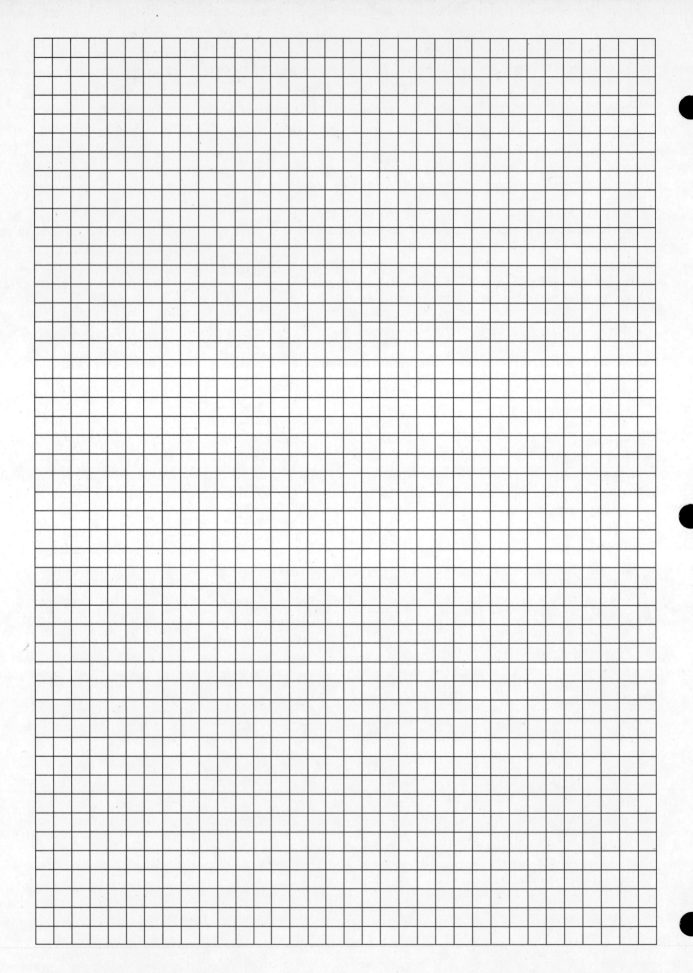

1 〜〜 Physics Lab

Egg Drop Project

Problem

Instruments destined to explore Mars or the moon must be packaged so that they are not damaged upon takeoff or landing. You and your partners will create a model for that package. You will design a container for an egg that will keep the egg from breaking when dropped from a height of approximately 5 m.

Procedure

1. Work with your group to think of several container designs that might protect an egg. Follow the restrictions below.

   - The design must allow easy opening and closing for egg inspection.
   - Before the container is dropped, it must fit into a 25-cm × 25-cm × 25-cm cube.
   - No liquids are allowed.
   - The egg must be raw, its shell uncoated.
   - The egg must survive a drop from approximately 5 m.
   - Designs with lower mass receive higher scores.

2. Decide which aspects of each idea should be incorporated into your final design.

3. Plan ahead. Set a timetable for experimentation, construction, testing, and redesigning if needed.

4. Make a list of materials you would like to use for your package.

5. Produce a detailed diagram or illustration of your container. Indicate which features you expect will contribute directly to the saftey of the egg.

6. Plan for a test drop of a few centimeters. If your egg breaks, revise your design. If you are satisfied with your design, continue.

7. Record the mass of your container (including egg).

8. Complete the actual egg drop. Inspect your egg. Give your container 10 points if the egg is unbroken, 5 points if the shell is cracked, $\frac{1}{2}$ point if the egg is broken. Find your score using the information below.

$$\text{Score} = \frac{2000}{\text{mass of container}} \times \text{earned egg points}$$

9. Dispose of the egg and materials with egg on them as instructed by your teacher. Clean and put away materials that can be reused.

Possible Materials

cushioning materials such as cotton balls, bubble wrap, balloons, and so on

tape, glue

raw egg

pan balance

3-m × 3-m square plastic drop cloth

paper towels and trash bags

1 Physics Lab

Analyze and Conclude

1. **Compare and Contrast** Which restriction did your team feel was the most limiting?

   _____

   _____

2. **Analyzing the Results** What was the most effective part of your design? What was the weakest part?

   _____

   _____

Apply

1. How would your container need to be redesigned so that it could safely carry two raw eggs?

   _____

   _____

Data and Observations

Table 1			
Group	Design	Container Mass	Score

1-1

Falling 👓

The Greek philosophers argued that heavy objects fall faster than light objects. Galileo stated that light and heavy objects fall at the same rate. What do you think? Drop four pennies taped together and a single penny from the same height at the same time. Tear a sheet of paper in half. Crumple one piece into a ball. Repeat your experiment with the paper ball and the half sheet of paper. What did you observe each time?

Analyze and Conclude

Who was correct, the Greeks or Galileo?

_____

_____

_____

_____

_____

_____

2 Design Your Own
Physics Lab

Mystery Plot

Problem

Can you accurately predict the unknown mass of an object by making measurements of other similar objects?

Hypothesis

Form a hypothesis that relates the mass of an object to another measurable quantity. Describe the variables to be measured and why these measurements are necessary.

_____

_____

_____

Possible Materials

4 pieces of electrical wire
   with lengths
   between 5 cm
   and 30 cm

3 rectangular pieces of
   floor tile

1 triangular piece of floor
   tile

metric ruler

balance

graph paper

Plan the Experiment

1. As a group, examine the pieces of floor tile and the pieces of electrical wire. Determine the quantities you want to measure. How can you assure the accuracy and precision of your measurements?

2. Identify the independent and dependent variables.

3. Which objects will be the unknown objects? Which objects will be measured? Set aside the unknowns.

4. Construct a data table or spreadsheet that will include all your measurements and calculations.

5. **Check the Plan** Make sure your teacher has approved your final plan before you proceed with your experiment.

6. Recycle and put away materials that can be reused when you are finished.

Analyze and Conclude

1. **Graphing Data** Make graphs of your measurements to observe relationships between variables. Clearly label the axes.

_____

_____

2 Physics Lab

2. **Analyzing Graphs** Identify the relationship between the variables. Do your graphs depict linear, quadratic, or inverse relationships? How do you know? Can you calculate the slope of each graph? Organize, analyze, evaluate, and make inferences in trends from your data. Predict from the trends in your data whether or not your graphs will go through the origin (0,0). Should they?

_____

_____

_____

3. **Calculating Results** Write the equations that relate your variables. Use the equations and the graphs to predict the unknown mass of wire and floor tile.

4. **Checking Your Hypothesis** Measure the unknown masses of the wire and floor tile on the balance. Do your measurements agree with the predicted values?

_____

_____

5. **Calculating Results** Use a computer plotting program or a graphing calculator to re-plot your data and find the equations that relate your variables. Are the equations the same as you found earlier?

_____

Apply

1. Suppose another group measures longer wires. How should the slope of your graph compare to their slope?

_____

_____

2. In the pharmaceutical industry, how might the weight of compressed medicine tablets be used to determine the quantity of finished tablets produced in a specific lot?

_____

_____

_____

_____

2-1   Pocket Lab

How good is your eye?

The distance from your nose to your outstretched fingertips is about 1 m. Estimate the distance between you and three objects in the room. Have the members in your lab group each make a data table and record their estimates. Verify each distance.

Compare Results

Were the estimates reasonably close? Did one person consistently make accurate estimates? What could be done to improve your accuracy?

_____

_____

_____

_____

_____

_____

_____

_____

_____

2-2

How far around?

Use a meterstick to measure the diameter of four circular objects and a string to measure their circumferences. Record your data in a table. Graph the circumference versus the diameter.

Communicate Results

Write a few sentences to summarize your graph. Write a sentence using the word that explains the meaning of the slope of your graph. Explain whether the value of the slope would be different if you had measured in different units.

_____

_____

_____

_____

_____

_____

_____

_____

_____

_____

3 WM Design Your Own Physics Lab

Notion of Motion

Problem

You are to construct motion diagrams based on a steady walk and a simulated sprint.

Hypothesis

Devise a procedure for creating motion diagrams for a steady walk and a sprint.

_____

_____

_____

Possible Materials

- stopwatch
- metersticks
- 10-m length of string, cord, or tape

Plan the Experiment

1. Decide on the variables to be measured and how you will measure them.
2. Decide how you will measure the distance over the course of the walk.
3. Create a data table.

Data and Observations				
Steady Walk				
distance				
time				
velocity				

4. Organize team members to perform the individual tasks of walker, sprinter, timekeeper, and recorder.
5. **Check the Plan** Make sure your teacher approves your final plan before you proceed.
6. Think about how the procedures you use for the fast sprint may differ from those you used for the steady walk, then follow steps **1–5**.
7. Dispose of, recycle, or put away materials as appropriate.

Analyze and Conclude

1. **Organizing Data** Use your data to write a word description of each event.

_____

_____

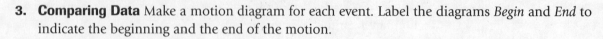

3 Physics Lab

2. **Comparing Results** Describe the data in the velocity portion of the WALK portion of the experiment. Then describe the data in the velocity portion of the SPRINT portion of the experiment.

_____

_____

3. **Comparing Data** Make a motion diagram for each event. Label the diagrams *Begin* and *End* to indicate the beginning and the end of the motion.

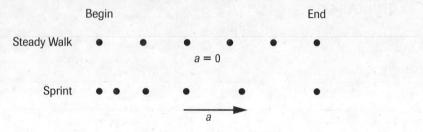

4. **Organizing Data** Draw the acceleration vectors on your motion diagram for the two events.

5. **Comparing Results** Compare the pattern of average velocity vectors for the two events. How are they different? Explain.

_____

_____

6. **Inferring Conclusions** Compare the acceleration vectors from the steady walk and the sprint. What can you conclude?

_____

_____

Apply

1. Imagine that you have a first-row seat for the 100-m world championship sprint. Write a description of the race in terms of velocity and acceleration. Include a motion diagram that would represent the race run by the winner.

_____

_____

Physics: Principles and Problems

3-1 Pocket Lab

Rolling Along

Tape a 2.5- to 3-m strip of paper to the floor or other smooth, level surface. Gently roll a smooth rubber or steel ball along the paper so that it takes about 4 or 5 s to cover the distance. Now roll the ball while a recorder makes beeps every 1.0 s. Mark the paper at the position of the rolling ball every 1.0 s.

Analyze and Conclude

Are the marks on the paper evenly spaced? Make a data table of position and time and use the data to plot a graph. In a few sentences, describe the graph.

_____

_____

_____

_____

_____

_____

_____

_____

Date _____   Period _____   Name _____

3-2

Swinging

Use a camcorder to capture an object swinging like a pendulum. Then attach a piece of tracing paper or other see-through material over the TV screen as you play back the video frame by frame.
Use a felt marker to show the position of the center of the swinging object at every frame as it moves from one side of the screen to the opposite side.

Analyze and Conclude

Does the object have a steady speed? Describe how the speed changes. Where is the object moving the fastest? Do you think that your results are true for other swinging objects? Why?

_____

_____

_____

_____

_____

_____

_____

_____

_____

_____

_____

_____

Physics: Principles and Problems

4  Physics Lab

The Paper River

Problem

How does a boat travel on a river?

Materials

small battery-powered car
  (or physics bulldozer)

meterstick

protractor

stopwatch

a piece of paper,
  1 m × 10 m

Procedure

1. Your car will serve as the boat. Write a brief statement to explain how the boat's speed can be determined.

   _____

   _____

   _____

2. Your boat will start with all wheels on the paper river. Measure the width of the river and predict how much time is needed for your boat to go directly across the river. Show your data and calculations.

3. Determine the time needed to cross the river when your boat is placed on the edge of the river. Make three trials and record the times.

4. Using the average of your trials, construct a graph showing the position and time for the boat crossing the river. If possible, use a computer or calculator to create the graph. Use this graph to observe and identify the relationship between variables.

5. Do you think it will take the boat more or less time to cross when the river is flowing? Explain your prediction.

   _____

   _____

6. Have a student (the hydro engineer) walk slowly, at a constant speed, while pulling the river along the floor. Each group should measure the time it takes for the boat to cross the flowing river. Make three trials and record the times. Compare the results with your prediction.

   _____

7. Using the grid from Step 4 and the average of your data from Step 6, construct a graph showing the position and time for the boat crossing the river when the river is flowing. Use a different color for the plot than you did for the boat without the river flowing.

4 Physics Lab

8. Devise a method to measure the speed of the river. Have the hydro engineer pull the river at a constant speed and collect the necessary data.

_____

9. Save the paper for later classes to use or recycle it.

Data and Observations

Table 1			
Moving River			
Trial #	Time (s)	Trial #	Time (s)

1. Does the boat move in the direction that it is pointing?

_____

_____

2. Analyze and evaluate the trends in your data. How did the graphs of position versus time compare?

_____

3. Infer from the trends in your data if the motion of the water affected the time needed to cross when the boat was pointed straight to the far shore.

_____

_____

_____

4. Based on the trends in your data, predict whether the river or the boat had the greater speed. Explain your choice.

_____

_____

Analyze and Conclude

1. **Calculating Results** Calculate the speed of the river.

4 Physics Lab

2. **Inferring Conclusions** Using your results for the speed of the boat and the speed of the river, calculate the speed of the boat compared to the ground when the boat is headed directly downstream and directly upstream.

Apply

1. Do small propeller aircraft always move in the direction that they are pointing? Do they ever fly sideways?

_____

_____

_____

_____

_____

2. Try the lab again using a battery-powered boat on a small stream.

_____

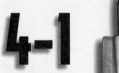 

Ladybug

You notice a ladybug moving from one corner of your textbook to the corner diagonally opposite. The trip takes the ladybug 6.0 s. Use the long side of the book as the *x*-axis. Find the component vectors of the ladybug's velocity, v_x and v_y, and the resultant velocity *R*.

Analyze and Conclude

Does the ladybug's path from one corner to the other affect the values in your measurements or calculations? Do $v_x + v_y$ really add up to *R*? Explain.

_____

_____

_____

_____

_____

_____

_____

_____

_____

_____

5 〰 Design Your Own Physics Lab

Ball and Car Race

Problem

A car moving along a highway passes a parked police car with a radar detector. Just as the car passes, the police car starts to pursue, moving with a constant acceleration. The police car catches up with the car just as it leaves the jurisdiction of the police officer.

Hypothesis

Sketch the position-versus-time graphs and the velocity-versus-time graphs for this chase, then simulate the chase.

Possible Materials

battery-powered car
1-in. steel ball
masking tape
stopwatch
wood block
graph paper
90-cm-long grooved track

Plan the Experiment

1. Identify the variables in this activity.
2. Determine how you will give the ball a constant acceleration.
3. Devise a method to ensure that both objects reach the end of the track at the same time.
4. Construct a data table that will show the positions of both objects at the beginning, the halfway point, and the end of the chase.
5. **Check the Plan** Review your plan with your teacher before you begin the race.
6. Construct *p-t* and *v-t* graphs for both objects. Use technology to construct these graphs if possible. Identify the relationships between variables.
7. Dispose of materials that cannot be reused or recycled. Put away materials that can be used again.

5 Physics Lab

Analyze and Conclude

1. **Comparing and Contrasting** Compare the velocities of the cars at the beginning and at the end of the chase. Write a verbal description.

_____

_____

_____

2. **Using Graphs** At any time during the chase, did the cars ever have the same velocity? If so, mark these points on the graphs.

_____

3. **Comparing and Contrasting** Compare the average velocity of the police car to that of the car.

_____

_____

4. **Calculating Results** Calculate the average speed of each car.

Apply

1. Explain why it took the police car so long to catch the car after it sped by.

_____

_____

_____

2. Analyze and evaluate the plots of the speeder's motion. Infer from the plots the speeder's acceleration.

_____

3. If the speeder accelerated at the exact same rate of the police car at the moment the speeder passes the police car, would the police car ever catch the speeder? Predict how your graphs would change.

_____

_____

4. Develop a CBL lab that plots velocity of a non-accelerated object and an accelerated object. Describe your graphs.

_____

Physics: Principles and Problems

5-1

Pocket Lab

Uniform or Not?

Set up a U-channel on a book so that it acts as an inclined ramp, or make a channel from two meter-sticks taped together along the edges. Release a steel ball so that it rolls down the ramp. Using a stop-watch, measure the time it takes the ball to roll 0.40 m.

Analyze and Conclude

Write a brief description of the motion of the ball. Predict how much time it would take the ball to roll 0.80 m. Explain your prediction.

_____

_____

_____

_____

_____

_____

_____

_____

_____

_____

5-2

 **Pocket Lab**

A Ball Race

Assemble an inclined ramp from a piece of U-channel or two metersticks taped together. Make a mark at 40 cm from the top and another at 80 cm from the top. If two balls are released at the same instant, one ball from the top and the other ball at 40 cm, will the balls get closer or farther apart as they roll down the ramp? Why? Try it. Now, release one ball from the top and then release another ball from the top as soon as the first ball reaches the 40-cm mark.

Analyze and Conclude

Explain your observations in terms of velocities. Do the balls ever have the same velocities as they roll down the hill? Do they have the same acceleration?

_____

_____

_____

_____

_____

_____

_____

_____

_____

_____

5-3

 Pocket Lab

Bowling Ball Displacement

Take a bowling ball and three stopwatches into the hallway. Divide into three groups. Have all timers start their watches when the ball is rolled. Group 1 should stop its watch when the ball has gone 10 m, group 2 should stop its watch when the ball has rolled 20 m, and group 3 should stop its watch when the ball has rolled 30 m.

Analyze and Conclude

Record the data and calculate the average speed for each distance. Could the average speed for 30 m be used to predict the time needed to roll 100 m? Why or why not?

_____

_____

_____

_____

_____

_____

_____

_____

5-4  Pocket Lab

Direction of Acceleration

Tape a bubble level onto the top of a laboratory cart. Center the bubble. Observe the direction of the motion of the bubble as you pull the cart forward, move it at constant speed, and allow it to coast to a stop. Relate the motion of the bubble to the acceleration of the cart. Predict what would happen if you tie the string to the back of the cart and repeat the experiment. Try it.

Analyze and Conclude

Draw motion diagrams for the cart as you moved it in the forward direction and it coasted to a stop and as you repeated the experiment in the opposite direction.

6 〰️ Physics Lab

The Elevator Ride

Problem

Why do you feel heavier or lighter when riding in an elevator?

Materials

1-kg mass
20-N spring scale
10 cm masking tape

Procedure

1. Imagine that you take an upward elevator ride. Write a few sentences describing when you feel normal, heavier than normal, and lighter than normal. Repeat for a downward elevator ride.

   _____

   _____

   _____

   _____

   _____

2. Hold the 1-kg mass in your hand and give it an upward elevator ride. Describe when the mass feels normal, heavier than normal, and lighter than normal.

   _____

   _____

   _____

   _____

3. Hold the mass in your hand and give it a downward elevator ride. Describe when the mass feels normal, heavier than normal, and lighter than normal.

   _____

   _____

   _____

4. Securely tape the mass to the hook on the spring scale.
   CAUTION: *A falling mass can cause serious damage to feet or toes.*

5. Start with the mass just above the floor and take it on an upward and then a downward elevator ride.

6. When complete, unwrap the tape and throw it away. Put away the mass and the spring scale.

Copyright © by Glencoe/McGraw-Hill

6 Physics Lab

Data and Observations

Table 1			
Place in the Ride	**Scale Reading (N)**	**Place in the Ride**	**Scale Reading (N)**

1. Watch the spring scale and record the readings for different parts of the ride.

Analyze and Conclude

1. **Interpreting Data** Identify those places in the ride when the spring scale records a normal value for the mass. Describe the motion of the mass. Are the forces balanced or unbalanced?

_____

_____

_____

_____

_____

_____

_____

2. **Interpreting Data** Identify those places in the ride when the spring scale records a heavier value. Which direction is the F_{net}? Which direction is the acceleration?

_____

_____

_____

_____

_____

_____

Name _____

6 Physics Lab

3. **Interpreting Data** Identify those places in the ride when the spring scale records a lighter value. Which direction is the F_{net}? Which direction is the acceleration?

_____

_____

_____

_____

_____

Apply

1. Based on the trends in your data, predict how riding in an elevator while standing on a scale will affect your weight measurement. Try it, and describe the forces on you.

_____

_____

_____

_____

2. Do you feel heavier or lighter when riding on an escalator? Explain your answer in terms of the motion and the forces.

_____

_____

_____

_____

_____

3. Identify the places on a roller coaster where you feel heavier or lighter. Explain your answer in terms of the motion and the forces.

_____

_____

_____

_____

_____

Physics: Principles and Problems

Copyright © by Glencoe/McGraw-Hill

Physics Lab and Pocket Lab Worksheets **25**

6-1

How far is forever?

Galileo proposed that if a perfectly smooth ball were rolled on a perfectly smooth surface in a vacuum, it would roll forever at a steady speed. Use a stopwatch with a lap or split timer and measure the time it takes a ball to roll the first meter and then the total time it takes to roll 2.0 m.

Analyze and Conclude

Make a motion diagram to describe the motion and a free-body diagram showing the forces acting on the ball. Indicate the direction of the net force, F_{net}, and the acceleration.

Physics: Principles and Problems

6-2

Pocket Lab

Tug-of-War Challenge

In a tug-of-war, predict how the force you exert on your end of the rope compares to the force your opponent exerts if you pull and your opponent just holds the end of the rope. Predict how the forces compare if the rope moves in your direction. Try it.

Analyze and Conclude

What did you notice about the forces? What happened when you started to move your opponent in your direction?

_____

_____

_____

_____

_____

_____

_____

_____

Friction depends on what?

Find out! Tape a 0.5-kg mass to a 10-cm × 10-cm piece of cardboard. Tie one end of a string to the mass and the other end to a spring scale. Pull until the mass begins to move. Record the maximum force before the mass began to slide as the static force of friction. Repeat for a 1.0-kg mass. Repeat with the two masses on a 10-cm × 20-cm piece of cardboard.

Analyze and Conclude

Describe your results. Does the force of friction depend on the mass? Does the force of friction depend on the surface area?

_____

_____

_____

_____

_____

_____

_____

_____

_____

_____

_____

6-4

Upside-Down Parachute

How long does it take for a falling object to reach a terminal velocity? How fast is the terminal velocity? Does the terminal velocity depend on the mass? Find out. Use coffee filters, a meterstick, a stopwatch, and your creativity to answer each question.

Analyze and Conclude

Describe your procedures, results, and conclusions to the class.

_____

_____

_____

_____

_____

_____

_____

_____

_____

_____

_____

_____

_____

_____

_____

_____

_____

_____

_____

_____

_____

_____

6-5

Stopping Forces

Tie two 1-m long strings to the backs of two lab carts and attach 0.2 kg masses to the other ends. Hang the masses over the end of a lab table so that the masses are just above the floor. Add mass to one of the carts so that its mass is about twice its original mass. Predict how the motion of the carts might be different when you push them at the same speed and then let them coast. Try it. Predict how you could change the mass on one of the strings so that the motion of the carts would be the same when given the same initial speed. Test your prediction.

Analyze and Conclude

Describe your observations in words and in a motion diagram. Explain your results in terms of inertia, force, mass, and acceleration.

_____

_____

_____

_____

_____

_____

_____

_____

7 〰〰 Design Your Own Physics Lab

The Softball Throw

Problem

What advice can you give the center fielder on your softball team on how to throw the ball to the catcher at home plate so that it gets there before the runner?

Hypothesis

Formulate a hypothesis using what you know about the horizontal and vertical motion of a projectile to advise the center fielder about how to throw the ball. Consider the factors that affect the time it will take for the ball to arrive at home plate.

_____

_____

_____

_____

Possible Materials

stopwatch

softball

football field or large open area with premeasured distances

Plan the Experiment

1. As a group, determine the variable(s) you want to measure. How do horizontal and vertical velocity affect the range?

2. Who will time the throws? How will you determine the range? Will the range be a constant or a variable? How many trials will you complete?

3. Construct a data table or spreadsheet for recording data from all the trial throws. Record all your calculations in a table.

Data and Observations

Table 1				
Range (*R*) (meters)	Time (*t*) (seconds)	Horizontal Velocity (v_x)(m/s)	Vertical Velocity (v_y) (m/s)	Initial Velocity (v_0) (m/s)
Trial 1				
Trial 2				

4. **Check the Plan** Make sure your teacher approves your final plan before you proceed.

7 Physics Lab

Analyze and Conclude

1. **Analyzing Data** How can your data be used to determine values for v_x and v_y?

2. **Diagramming the Results** Draw a diagram that shows the relationship between R, v_x, v_y, and v_0.

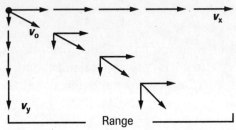

This diagram assumes that the ball is thrown straight forward.

3. **Calculating Results** Determine the initial values for v_x and v_y. Use the Pythagorean theorem to find the value of the initial velocity, v_0, for each trial.

4. **Analyzing Data** Was the range of each person's throw about the same? Did the initial velocity of the throws vary?

   _____

5. **Analyzing Data** Analyze and evaluate the trends in your data. How did the angle at which the ball was thrown affect the range? The time?

   _____

   _____

   _____

6. **Checking Your Hypothesis** Should the center fielder throw the ball to the catcher at home plate with a larger v_x or v_y?

   _____

   _____

Apply

1. Infer from the trends in your data why a kickoff in a football game might be made at a different angle than a punt.

   _____

   _____

7-1

Over the Edge

Obtain two balls, one twice the mass of the other. Predict which ball will hit the floor first when you roll them over the surface of a table with the same speed and let them roll off. Predict which ball will hit the floor farther from the table. Explain your predictions.

_____

_____

_____

_____

_____

_____

_____

Analyze and Conclude

Does the mass of the ball affect its motion? Is mass a factor in any of the equations for projectile motion?

_____

_____

_____

_____

_____

_____

7-2

Pocket Lab

Where the Ball Bounces

Place a golf ball in your hand and extend your arm sideways so that the ball is at shoulder height. Drop the ball and have a lab partner start a stopwatch when the ball strikes the floor and stop it the next time the ball strikes the floor. Predict where the ball will hit when you walk at a steady speed and drop the ball. Would the ball take the same time to bounce? Try it.

Analyze and Conclude

Where does the ball hit? Does it take more time?

_____

_____

_____

_____

_____

_____

_____

7-3

Target Practice

Tie a 1.0-m length of string onto a one-hole rubber stopper. **Note:** Everyone in the classroom should be wearing goggles. Swing the stopper around your head in a horizontal circle. Release the string from your hand when the string is lined up with a spot on the wall. Repeat the experiment until the stopper flies toward the spot on the wall.

Analyze and Conclude

Did the stopper travel toward the spot on the wall? What does this indicate about the direction of the velocity compared to the orientation of the string?

_____

_____

_____

_____

_____

_____

_____

_____

7-4

Falling Sideways

Will a ball dropped straight down hit the floor before or after a ball that is tossed directly sideways at the same instant? Try it. You may need to repeat the experiment several times before you are sure of your results. Toss the ball sideways and not up or down.

Analyze and Conclude

Compare the downward force on each ball. Compare the distance that each ball falls in the vertical direction.

_____

_____

_____

_____

_____

_____

_____

_____

8 〰 Physics Lab

The Orbit

Problem

How does the gravitational force vary at different points of an elliptical orbit?

Materials

[icons]

2 pushpins

21-cm × 28-cm piece of cardboard or corkboard

sheet of paper

30-cm piece of string or thread

pencil

metric ruler

Procedure

1. Place the paper on top of the cardboard. Push the pushpins into the paper and cardboard so that they are between 7 and 10 cm apart.

2. Make a loop with the string. Place the loop over the two pushpins. Keep the loop tight as you draw the ellipse, as shown on page 179 in your textbook.

3. Remove the pins and string. Draw a small star centered at one of the pinholes.

4. Draw the position of a planet in the orbit where it is farthest from the star. Measure and record the distance from this position to the center of the star.

5. Draw a 1-cm-long force vector from this planet directly toward the star. Label this vector 1.0 *F*.

6. Draw the position of a planet when it is nearest the star. Measure and record the distance from this position to the star's center.

Data and Observations

Table 1	
Farthest Distance	
Nearest Distance	

Analyze and Conclude

1. **Calculating Results** Calculate the amount of force on the planet at the closest distance. Gravity is an inverse square force. If the planet is 0.45 times as far as the closest distance, the force is $1/(0.45)^2$ as much, or 4.9 *F*. **Hint:** The force will be more than 1.0 *F*.

8 Physics Lab

2. **Diagramming Results** Draw the force vector, using the correct length and direction, for this position and at two other positions in the orbit. Use the scale 1.0 F : 1.0 cm.

Apply

1. Draw a velocity vector at each planet position to show the direction of motion. Assume that the planet moves in a clockwise pattern on the ellipse. Predict where the planet moves fastest. Use an orbital motion simulation program for a computer to verify your prediction.

_____

_____

2. Look at the direction of the velocity vectors and the direction of the force vectors at each position of the planet. Infer where the planet gains and loses speed. Explain your reasoning.

_____

_____

_____

8-1

Pocket Lab

Strange Orbit

Does the moon affect the motion of Earth in its orbit around the sun? Make your prediction. Then, build the following model planet and moon system. Push a small ball of clay onto the end of a drinking straw to represent the moon. Push a larger ball of clay, representing the planet, onto the opposite end. Tape a piece of string to the balance point on the straw so that the straw will stay parallel to the table when it is lifted. Give the moon a gentle push so that it moves in a slow circle.

Analyze and Conclude

Does the planet move in response to the motion of the moon? What effect would a more massive moon have on the planet? What might you conclude about Earth's motion?

_____

_____

_____

_____

_____

_____

_____

_____

_____

_____

8-2  Pocket Lab

Weight in a Free Fall

Tie a string to the top of a spring scale. Hang a 1.0-kg mass on the spring scale. Hold the scale in your hand.

Analyze and Conclude

Observe the weight of the mass. What will the reading be when the string is released (as the mass and scale are falling)? Why?

_____

_____

_____

_____

_____

_____

_____

8-3  Pocket Lab

Water, Water, Everywhere

This activity is best done outdoors. Use a pencil to poke a hole in the bottom and side of a cup. Hold your fingers over the two holes as you pour colored water into the cup until it is two-thirds full. Predict what will happen as the cup is allowed to fall. Drop the cup and watch closely.

Analyze and Conclude

What happened? Why?

_____

_____

_____

_____

_____

_____

_____

_____

_____

_____

_____

_____

_____

9 〰️ Physics Lab

The Explosion

Problem

How do the forces and changes in momenta acting on different masses compare during an explosion?

Materials

two laboratory carts
(one with a spring
mechanism)

two C-clamps

two blocks of wood

20-N spring balance

0.50-kg mass

stopwatch

masking tape

meterstick

Procedure

1. Securely tape the 0.50-kg mass to cart 2 and then use the balance to determine the mass of each cart.

2. Use the C-clamps to secure the two blocks of wood to the laboratory table. Position the blocks at least 1 m apart.

3. Arrange the equipment as shown in the diagram.

4. Predict the starting position so that the carts will hit the blocks at the same instant when the spring mechanism is released.

5. Place pieces of tape on the table at the front of the carts to mark starting positions.

6. Depress the mechanism to release the spring and explode the carts.

7. Notice which cart hits the block first.

8. Adjust the starting position for the carts until they hit the wood blocks at the same time. Be sure to mark the starting position of each cart for each trial. Measure the time it takes the carts to reach the blocks.

9. Dispose of the masking tape and put the other materials away.

Data and Observations

1. Which cart moved farther? How do you know?

   _____

   _____

2. Which cart moved faster? Explain.

   _____

   _____

Analyze and Conclude

1. **Analyzing** Which data will help you estimate the velocity of each cart? Explain.

   _____

   _____

9 Physics Lab

2. **Estimating** Which cart had the greater velocity?

_____

_____

3. **Comparing** Compare the change in momentum of each cart.

_____

_____

4. **Applying** Suppose that the spring pushed on cart 1 for 0.05 s. How long did cart 2 push on the spring? Explain.

_____

_____

5. **Comparing** Using $F\Delta t = m\Delta v$, which cart had the greater impulse?

_____

_____

Apply

1. Based on your data, explain why a target shooter might prefer to shoot a more massive gun.

_____

_____

_____

_____

9-1

 *Pocket Lab*

Cart Momentum

Attach a spring scale to a laboratory cart. First, pull the cart for 1.0 s while exerting 1.0 N of force. Next, pull the cart for 2.0 s while exerting about 0.50 N of force. Predict which trial will give the cart more acceleration. Explain.

_____

_____

Predict which trial will give the cart more velocity. Explain.

_____

_____

Then try it.

Recognizing Cause and Effect

Which factor, F or Δt, seems to be more important in changing the velocity of the cart?

_____

_____

_____

_____

_____

_____

9-2

Skateboard Fun

Have two students sit facing each other on skateboards approximately 3 to 5 m apart. Place a rope in their hands. Predict what will happen when one student pulls on the rope while the other just holds his or her end. Explain your prediction. Which person is exerting more force on the rope?

_____

_____

_____

Compare the amount of time that the force is acting on each person. Which person will have a greater change in momentum? Explain.

_____

_____

_____

Then try it. Describe what really happened.

_____

_____

_____

Design an Experiment

Can you devise a method to pull only one student to the other so that the other student doesn't move?

_____

_____

_____

_____

_____

_____

_____

_____

10 〰〰 Design Your Own
Physics Lab

Your Power

Problem

Can you estimate the power that you generate as you climb stairs? Climbing stairs requires energy. As you move your weight through a distance, you accomplish work. The rate at which you do this work is power.

Hypothesis

Form a hypothesis that relates estimating power to measurable quantities. Predict the difficulties you may encounter as you are trying to solve the problem.

_____

_____

_____

_____

Possible Materials

Determine which variables you will measure and then plan a procedure for taking measurements. Tell your teacher what materials you would like to use to accomplish your plan. Once you have completed your lab, be sure to dispose of, recycle, or put away your materials.

Plan the Experiment

In your group, develop a plan to measure your power as you climb stairs. Be prepared to present your plan, your data, your calculations, and your results to the rest of the class. Take measurements for at least two students.

1. Identify the dependent and independent variables.

2. Describe your procedures.

3. Set up data tables.

4. Write any equations that you will need for the calculations.

5. **Check the Plan** Show your teacher your plan before you leave the room to start the experiment.

Analyze and Conclude

1. **Calculating Results** Show your calculations for the power rating of each climber.

10 Physics Lab

2. **Comparing Results** Did each climber have the same power rating?

_____

_____

_____

3. **Analyzing Data** Explain how your power could be increased.

_____

_____

_____

_____

4. **Making Inferences** Explain why the fastest climber might not have the highest power rating. Explain why the largest climber might not have the highest power rating.

_____

_____

_____

_____

Apply

1. Your local electric company charges you about 11 cents for a kilowatt-hour of energy. At this rate, how much money could you earn by climbing stairs continuously for one hour? Show your calculations.

10-1

Pocket Lab

Working Out

Attach a spring scale to a 1.0-kg mass with a string. Pull the mass along the table at a slow, steady speed while keeping the scale parallel to the tabletop. Note the reading on the spring scale.

Analyze and Conclude

What are the physical factors that determine the amount of force? How much work is done in moving the mass 1.0 m? Predict the force and the work when a 2.0-kg mass is pulled along the table. Try it. Was your prediction accurate?

_____

_____

_____

_____

_____

_____

_____

_____

_____

_____

_____

_____

10-2

An Inclined Mass

Attach a spring scale to a 1.0-kg mass with a string. Increase the angle between the string and the table-top, for example, to 30°. Try to keep the angle constant as you pull the 1.0-kg mass along the table at a slow, steady speed. Note the reading on the scale.

Analyze and Conclude

How much force is in the direction of motion? How much work is done when the 1.0-kg mass moves 1.0 m? How does the work compare to the previous value?

_____

_____

_____

_____

_____

_____

_____

_____

_____

_____

_____

_____

10-3

 *Pocket Lab*

Wheel and Axle

The gear mechanism on your bicycle multiplies the distance that you travel. What does it do to the force? Try this activity to find out. Mount a wheel and axle on a solid support rod. Wrap a string clockwise around the small diameter wheel and a different string counterclockwise around the large diameter wheel. Hang a 500-g mass from the end of the string on the larger wheel. Pull the string down so that the mass is lifted by about 10 cm.

Analyze and Conclude

What did you notice about the force on the string in your hand? What did you notice about the distance that your hand needed to move to lift the mass? Explain the results in terms of the work done on both strings.

_____

_____

_____

_____

_____

_____

_____

_____

_____

_____

_____

11 Design Your Own Physics Lab

Down the Ramp

Problem

What factors affect the speed of a cart at the bottom of a ramp? Along the floor?

Hypothesis

Form a hypothesis that relates the speed or energy of the cart at the bottom of the ramp to the mass of the cart on the ramp.

_____

_____

_____

_____

_____

Possible Materials

cart

0.50-kg mass

1.0-kg mass

board to be used as a ramp

stopwatch

meterstick

masking tape

Plan the Experiment

1. Your lab group should develop a plan to answer the questions stated in the problem. How should you structure your investigation? How many trials do you need for each setup? Be prepared to present and defend your plan, data, and results to the class.

2. Identify the independent and dependent variables. Which will you keep constant?

3. Describe your procedures.

4. Describe the energy changes as the cart rolls down the ramp and onto the floor.

5. Construct data tables or spreadsheets that will show the measurements that you make.

6. **Check the Plan** Make sure your teacher has approved your plan before you proceed with your experiment.

7. When you have completed the lab, dispose of, recycle, or put away your materials.

11 Physics Lab

Analyze and Conclude

1. **Checking Your Hypothesis** Did the speed at the bottom of the ramp depend on the mass of the cart? Does twice the mass have twice the speed? Does three times the mass go three times as fast?

   _____

   _____

2. **Calculating Results** List and explain the equations that you used for your energy calculations. What do the equations suggest about the speed at the bottom when the mass is changed?

   _____

   _____

   _____

3. **Comparing and Contrasting** Compare the gravitational potential energy of the cart at the starting position to the kinetic energy of the cart along the floor. What is your conclusion?

   _____

   _____

4. **Thinking Critically** Suppose one lab group finds that the cart has 30% more kinetic energy along the floor than the starting gravitational potential energy. What would you tell the group?

   _____

   _____

Apply

1. A Soap Box Derby is a contest in which riders coast down a long hill. Does the mass of the cart have a significant effect on the results? Predict what other factors may be more important in winning the race.

   _____

   _____

   _____

   _____

Energy in Coins

Does your car require more or less stopping distance when it is loaded with passengers than when you are driving alone? A short activity will help you to answer this question. Lay a ruler on a smooth table. Place two quarters against the edge of the ruler. Momentarily push the two quarters at the same speed across the table, and then stop the ruler. The two quarters should slide the same distance before stopping. Now tape another coin on top of one quarter to increase its mass. Again push the coins with the ruler.

Analyze and Conclude

Does the stopping distance depend upon the mass? Explain.

_____

_____

_____

_____

_____

_____

_____

_____

_____

_____

_____

11-2

Energy Exchange

Wear goggles for this activity. Select several different-sized steel balls and determine their masses. Stand a spring-loaded laboratory cart on end with the spring mechanism pointing upward. Place a ball on top of the spring mechanism. Press down on the ball to compress the spring until the ball is touching the cart. Quickly release the ball so that the spring shoots it upward. Repeat several times and measure the average height. Predict how high the other sizes of steel balls should go. Try it. Record the values in a data table.

Analyze and Conclude

Classify the balls in order of height attained. What conclusions can you reach?

_____

_____

_____

_____

_____

_____

_____

_____

_____

_____

12 Physics Lab

Heating Up

Problem

How does a constant supply of thermal energy affect the temperature of water?

Materials

hot plate (or Bunsen burner)

250-mL ovenproof glass beaker

water

thermometer

stopwatch

goggles

apron

Procedure

1. Turn your hot plate to a medium setting (or as recommended by your teacher). Allow a few minutes for the plate to heat up. Wear goggles.

2. Pour 150 mL of room-temperature water into the 250-mL beaker.

3. Make a data and observations table.

4. Record the initial temperature of the water. The thermometer must not touch the bottom or sides of the beaker.

5. Place the beaker on the hot plate and record the temperature every 1.0 min. Carefully stir the water before taking a temperature reading.

6. Record the time when the water starts to boil. Continue recording the temperature for an additional 4.0 min.

7. Carefully remove the beaker from the hot plate. Record the temperature of the remaining water.

8. When you have completed the lab, dispose of the water as instructed by your teacher. Allow equipment to cool before putting it away.

Data and Observations

Table 1					
Time	Temperature	Time	Temperature	Time	Temperature

Analyze and Conclude

1. **Analyzing Data** Make a graph of temperature (vertical axis) versus time (horizontal axis). Use a computer or a calculator to construct the graph if possible. What is the relationship between variables?

Sample graph:

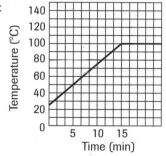

12 Physics Lab

Name _____

2. **Interpreting Graphs** What is the slope of the graph for the first 3.0 minutes? Be sure to include units.

3. **Relating Concepts** What is the thermal energy given to the water in the first 3.0 minutes? Hint: $Q = mC\Delta T$.

4. **Making Predictions** Use a dotted line on the same graph to predict what the graph would look like if the same procedure was followed with only half as much water.

Apply

1. Would you expect that the hot plate transferred energy to the water at a steady rate?

_____

_____

2. Where is the energy going when the water is boiling?

_____

_____

_____

Copyright © by Glencoe/McGraw-Hill

Physics: Principles and Problems

12-1

Pocket Lab

Melting

Label two foam cups *A* and *B*. Measure 75 mL of room-temperature water into each of the two cups. Add an ice cube to cup A. Add ice water to cup B until the water levels are equal. Measure the temperature of each cup at 1-min intervals until the ice has melted.

Analyze and Conclude

Do the samples reach the same final temperature? Why?

_____

_____

_____

_____

_____

_____

_____

_____

_____

_____

12-2  *Pocket Lab*

Cool Times

Place a 100-mL beaker in a 250-mL beaker. Put a thermometer in each beaker. Fill the small beaker with hot, colored water. Determine the temperature of the colored water. Slowly pour tap water into the large beaker until the water is at the same height in both beakers. Record the temperature in the large beaker. Record the temperature in both beakers every minute for 5 min. Plot your data for both beakers on a graph of temperature versus time. Measure and record the mass of water in each beaker.

Calculate and Conclude

Predict the final temperature. Describe each curve.

_____

_____

_____

_____

_____

_____

_____

_____

_____

_____

_____

Date _____   Period _____   Name _____

12-3   *Pocket Lab*

Drip, Drip, Drip

Measure equal amounts of very hot and very cold water into two clear glasses (or beakers).

Hypothesize and Test

Predict what will happen if you simultaneously put one drop of food coloring in each glass. Try it. What happened? Why? Was the mixing symmetric?

_____

_____

_____

_____

_____

_____

_____

_____

_____

_____

_____

_____

13 〰〰 Physics Lab

Float or Sink?

Problem

How can you measure the buoyancy of objects?

Materials

beaker

water

film canister with lid

25 pennies

250-g spring scale

pan balance

Procedure

1. Measure and calculate the volume of a film canister. Record the volume in a data table like the one shown.

2. Fill the canister with water. Find the mass of the filled canister on the pan balance. Record the value in your data table.

3. Empty the canister of water.

4. Place a few pennies in the canister and put the top on tightly. Find its mass and record the value in your data table.

5. Put the capped film canister into a beaker of water to see if it floats.

6. If it floats, estimate the percentage that is under water. Record this amount in your data table.

7. If it sinks, use the spring scale to measure the apparent weight while it is under water (but not touching the bottom). Record this value in your data table.

8. Repeat steps 4 through 7 using different numbers of pennies for each trial.

9. Calculate the density for each trial in g/cm³.

10. Dispose of the water as instructed by your teacher. Dry wet materials before putting them away.

Data and Observations

Table 1		
Volume of canister = _____ cm³		
Mass of canister with water = _____ g		
Floaters		
Mass with pennies	% below water	Density
Sinkers		
Mass with pennies	Apparent weight	Density

13 Physics Lab

Analyze and Conclude

1. **Recognizing Spatial Relationships** Look closely at the mass of the floaters and the percentages below the water. What seems to be the rule?

_____

_____

_____

_____

2. **Comparing and Contrasting** Look closely at the sinkers. How much lighter are the canisters when weighed under water?

_____

_____

_____

Apply

1. Explain why a steel-hulled boat can float, even though it is quite massive.

_____

_____

_____

2. Icebergs float in salt water (density 1.03 g/cm^3) with 1/9 of their volume above water. What is the density of an iceberg?

13-1  Pocket Lab

Foot Pressure

How much pressure do you exert when standing on the ground with one foot? Is it more or less than air pressure? Estimate your weight in newtons. **Hint:** 500 N = 110 lb. Stand on a piece of paper and have a lab partner trace the outline of your foot. Draw a rectangle that has about the same area as the outline.

Using SI Measurement

Calculate the area of your rectangle in square meters, and use the definition of pressure to estimate your pressure. $P = F/A$.

13-2

Pocket Lab

Floating?

Pour water into a glass or small beaker until it is three-fourths full. Gently place a needle on the surface of the water. Try to float it. Then try to float a paper clip, a metal staple, or a steel razor blade.

Relate Cause and Effect

Explain your results.

_____

_____

_____

_____

_____

_____

_____

_____

_____

_____

13-3

 **Pocket Lab**

Jumpers

Put on a pair of safety goggles. Examine the jumping disk. Notice that it is slightly curved. Now rub the disk for several seconds until it becomes curved in the other direction. Place the disk on a flat, level surface and stand back.

Make a Hypothesis

Suggest a hypothesis that might explain the jumping. Suggest a method to test your hypothesis.

_____

_____

_____

_____

_____

_____

_____

_____

_____

_____

_____

_____

_____

_____

14 Design Your Own
Physics Lab

Waves on a Coiled Spring

Problem

How can you model the properties of transverse waves?

Hypothesis

A coiled spring toy can be used to model transverse waves and to investigate wave properties such as speed, frequency, amplitude, and wavelength.

Possible Materials

a long coiled spring toy

stopwatch

meterstick

Plan the Experiment

1. Work in pairs or groups, and clear a path of about 6 m for this activity.

2. One member of the team should grip the spring firmly with one hand. Another member of the team should stretch the spring to the length suggested by your teacher. Team members should take turns holding the end of the spring. **CAUTION:** *Coiled springs easily get out of control. Do not allow them to get tangled or overstretched.*

3. The second team member should then make a quick sideways snap of the wrist to produce transverse wave pulses. Other team members can assist in measuring, timing, and recording data. It is easier to see the motion from one end of the spring, rather than from the side.

4. Design experiments to answer the questions under Analyze and Conclude.

5. **Check the Plan** Make sure your teacher has approved your final plan before you proceed with your experiments.

Analyze and Conclude

1. **Interpreting Data** What happens to the amplitude of the transverse wave as it travels?

    _____

    _____

    _____

    _____

2. **Recognizing Cause and Effect** Does the transverse wave's speed depend upon its amplitude?

    _____

    _____

14 Physics Lab

3. **Observing and Interpreting** If you put two quick transverse wave pulses into the spring and consider the wavelength to be the distance between the pulses, does the wavelength change as the pulses move?

_____

_____

_____

4. **Applying** How can you decrease the wavelength of a transverse wave?

_____

_____

_____

5. **Interpreting** As transverse wave pulses travel back and forth on the spring, do they bounce off each other or pass through each other?

_____

_____

_____

Apply

1. How do the speeds of high frequency (short wavelength) transverse waves compare with the speeds of low frequency (long wavelength) transverse waves?

_____

_____

_____

_____

2. Suppose you designed the experiment using longitudinal waves. How would the procedure for longitudinal waves be different from the procedure for transverse waves?

_____

_____

3. Would you expect the results of an experiment with longitudinal waves to be similar to the results of the transverse wave experiment? Explain why or why not.

_____

_____

14-1 Pocket Lab

Wave Reflections

Waves lose amplitude and transfer energy when they reflect from a barrier. What happens to the speed of the waves? Use a wave tank with a projection system. Half-fill the tank with water. Dip your finger into the water near one end of the tank and notice how fast the wave that you make moves to the other end.

Analyze

Does the wave slow down as it travels? Use a stopwatch to measure the time for a wave to cover two lengths, then four lengths, of the wave tank.

_____

_____

_____

_____

_____

14-2

Wave Interaction

What happens to the waves coming from different directions when they meet? Do they slow down, bounce off each other, or go through each other?

Design an Experiment

Use a coiled spring toy to test these questions. Record your procedures and observations.

_____
_____
_____
_____
_____
_____
_____
_____
_____
_____

14-3

Bent Out of Shape

What happens to a water wave's speed when the depth of the water changes? How does a change in speed affect the shape of the waves? Try this activity to find out. Use a wave tank with a projection system. Adjust the tank so that the water is shallow on one side and deep on the opposite side. Dip your finger or pencil eraser into the middle of the tank, and gently tap the water to make a circular wave. Watch closely. Do the waves hit the sides of the tank at the same time? What happens to the wavelength in different directions?

Modeling

Make a sketch of the shape of the waves. Label the deep and shallow ends on your drawing. Describe the relationship between the depth of the water and the wave's speed (inverse or direct). What did you notice about the wavelength in different directions?

_____

_____

_____

_____

15 〰 Physics Lab

Speed of Sound

Problem
How can you measure the speed of sound?

Materials

🥽

tuning fork

hollow glass tube

1000-mL graduated
    cylinder

hot water

ice water

thermometer

tuning fork hammer

tape measure

Procedure

1. Place cylinders with hot water on one side of the classroom and ice water on the other side of the classroom.

2. Record the value of the frequency that is stamped on the tuning fork and record the temperature of the water.

3. Wear goggles while using tuning forks next to the glass tubes. With the tube lowered in the cylinder, carefully strike the tuning fork with the rubber hammer.

4. Hold the tuning fork above the glass tube while you slowly raise the tube until the sound is amplified, and is loudest by the tube.

5. Measure L, the distance from the water to the top of the tube, to the nearest 0.5 cm.

6. Trade places with another group on the other side of the room and repeat steps 2–5 using the same tuning fork.

7. Repeat steps 2–6 using a different tuning fork.

8. Dispose of the water as instructed by your teacher. Make sure materials are dry before you put them away.

Data and Observations

Table 1					
Hot Water					
Known	$f =$		Known	$f =$	
Measure	$T =$		Measure	$T =$	
	$L =$			$L =$	
Calculate	$\lambda =$		Calculate	$\lambda =$	
	$v =$			$v =$	
Cold Water					
Known	$f =$		Known	$f =$	
Measure	$T =$		Measure	$T =$	
	$L =$			$L =$	
Calculate	$\lambda =$		Calculate	$\lambda =$	
	$v =$			$v =$	

15 Physics Lab

Analyze and Conclude

1. **Calculating Results** Calculate the values for λ and *v*.

2. **Comparing Results** Were the values of *v* different for cold and hot air? How do the values of *v* compare for different tuning forks?

_____
_____
_____
_____

3. **Making Inferences** Write a general statement describing how the speed of sound depends on the variables tested in this experiment.

_____
_____
_____
_____

4. **Forming an Explanation** Describe a possible model of sound moving through air that will explain your results.

_____
_____
_____

Apply

1. What would an orchestra sound like if the higher frequencies traveled faster than the lower frequencies?

_____
_____
_____

15-1

Pocket Lab

Sound Off

Take a meterstick and tape recorder to the band room. Measure the entire length of a wind instrument. Ask a musician to play the lowest note possible on her instrument. Make a recording of the lowest note. Return to the physics room.

Analyze and Conclude

For the lowest note, $L = \lambda/2$, what is the wavelength played by the instrument? Use this estimate of the wavelength and the wave equation to predict the frequency. **Hint:** $v = \lambda f$. Use a frequency generator to try to match the recorded note. Read the value on the frequency generator. Is this reading close to your prediction?

_____

_____

_____

_____

_____

_____

15-2

Ring, Ring

How good is your hearing? Here is a simple test to find out. Find a penny, a nickel, a dime, and a quarter. Ask a lab partner to drop them in any order and listen closely. Can you identify the sound of each coin with your eyes closed?

Analyze and Conclude

Describe the differences in the sounds. What are the physical factors that cause the differences in the sounds? Can you suggest any patterns?

_____

_____

_____

_____

_____

_____

_____

_____

_____

_____

_____

_____

Date _____ Period _____ Name _____

16  Physics Lab

Light Ray Paths

Problem

How do light waves travel?

Materials

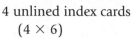

4 unlined index cards
(4 × 6)

clay

40-watt lightbulb
(nonfrosted) in a fixture

4–6 flat mirrors,
approximately
10 cm × 15 cm

medium nail

ruler

Procedure

1. Draw two diagonals on each index cards, using the ruler. Mark the center of each card.

2. Punch the center of three of the cards with the nail.

3. Stand one of the punched cards so that its longer edge is parallel to a desk or tabletop. Use two pea-sized lumps of clay to secure the card to the table.

4. Stand the remaining cards on the table so they are about 10 cm apart. Place the card without the hole last. Use clay to secure all the cards.

5. Arrange the cards so their outside edges are in a straight line. Use the ruler to check the alignment. Once your setup is complete, dim the room lights.

6. Ask your partner to hold the light fixture so the light shines through the hole in the first card.

7. Check the alignment of the two other punched cards so you can see the light shining on the fourth card.

8. Place a mirror in front of the fourth card so the light shines on it. Give each person in your group a mirror, and have them hold it in a position that reflects the light beam to the next person's mirror. Be careful not to reflect the light beam into someone's eye.

9. When you have completed the lab, recycle the index cards and save the clay for use again.

Data and Observations

1. Decide how to place the mirrors so that you can reflect the light onto the back of the card without the hole.

_____

_____

2. Draw a diagram showing your mirror setup. Use arrows to mark the path of light between the mirrors and the card.

_____

_____

Physics: Principles and Problems   *Physics Lab and Pocket Lab Worksheets* **79**

Copyright © by Glencoe/McGraw-Hill

16 Physics Lab

3. Describe how the brightness of the light shining on the first mirror compares with the brightness of the light reflected from the last mirror.

_____

_____

Analyze and Conclude

1. **Analyzing Data** How can you describe the path of light from one mirror to the next?

_____

_____

2. **Critical Thinking** What explanation can you give for your observations concerning the relative brightness of the reflections?

_____

_____

_____

_____

_____

Apply

1 Use your observations to draw a diagram showing how a shadow forms.

_____

_____

_____

16-1

Pocket Lab

An Illuminating Matter

Which is more efficient, or has the highest lm/W, a lower- or higher-power lightbulb? To find out, look at your lightbulbs at home and record the power and lumens for at least three different bulbs.

Graph Your Results

Make a graph of power (horizontal axis) versus lumens (vertical axis). Summarize your results.

_____

_____

_____

_____

_____

_____

_____

_____

16-2 Pocket Lab

Hot and Cool Colors

Some artists refer to red and orange as hot colors and green and blue as cool colors. But does emitting red or orange light really indicate that an object is hotter than one emitting blue or green? Try this to find out. Obtain a pair of prism glasses or a piece of diffraction grating from your teacher. Find a lamp with a dimmer switch and turn off the light. Next, slowly turn the dimmer so that the light gets brighter and brighter. To get the best effect, turn off all the other lights in the room.

Analyze and Conclude

Which colors appeared first when the light was dim? Which colors were the last to appear? How do these colors relate to the temperature of the filament?

_____

_____

_____

_____

_____

_____

_____

_____

_____

16-3

Pocket Lab

Soap Solutions

Dip a ring into soap solution and hold it at a 45° angle to the horizontal. Look for color bands to form in horizontal stripes.

Analyze and Conclude

Why do the bands move? Why are the bands horizontal? What type of pattern would you see if you looked through the soap with a red filter? Try it. Describe and explain your results.

_____

_____

_____

_____

_____

_____

_____

_____

_____

_____

16-4  Pocket Lab

Light Polarization

Obtain a polarizing filter from your teacher to take home. Look through the filter at various objects as you rotate the filter. Make a record of those objects that seem to change in brightness as the filter is rotated.

Recognize Cause and Effect

What seems to be the pattern?

_____

_____

_____

_____

_____

_____

17 〰〰 Physics Lab

Bending of Light

Problem

How is the index of refraction of light in water determined?

Procedure

Part I

1. Draw a line dividing the graph paper in half.

2. Use the felt-tip pen to draw a vertical line at the center of the straight edge of the plastic dish. This line will be your object.

3. Place the edge of the dish along the straight line so that the dish is on the bottom half of the paper. Trace the outline of the dish on the paper.

4. Mark the position of the object on your paper.

5. Add water until the dish is three-fourths full.

6. Lay a ruler on the bottom half of the paper. Adjust the position until the edge of the ruler seems to point at the object when you look through the water.

7. Have a lab partner check to verify that the ruler position is accurate.

8. Draw a line along the ruler edge to the edge of the dish.

9. Repeat steps **6–8** for a different position of the ruler.

Part II

1. Wipe the vertical line from the dish and draw a vertical line at the center of the curved edge. This is your new object.

2. Repeat all steps from Part I, but this time sight the ruler on the top half of the paper.

3. Dispose of the water as instructed by your teacher. Dry and put away materials that can be reused.

Materials

graph paper
felt-tip pen
ruler
semicircular plastic dish
water

Data and Observations

1. Look at the sight lines you drew in Part I. Did the light bend when moving from water to air?

   _____

   _____

2. For Part II, do the sight lines point directly toward the object?

   _____

   _____

17 Physics Lab

3. For Part II, draw a line from the object position to the point where each sight line touches the dish.

4. Draw the normal at each point where the sight line touched the dish.

5. Measure the angles from the normal for the angles in air and water.

Analyze and Conclude

1. **Interpreting Data** Explain why the light did not bend in Part I. (**Hint:** Draw the normal to the surface.)

_____

_____

_____

_____

_____

2. **Calculating Values** Calculate n, using Snell's law.

Apply

1. Could a flat piece of material be used for focusing light? Make a drawing to support your answer.

_____

_____

17-1

Pocket Lab

Reflections

Toss a tennis ball or a handball against a wall so that it will bounce to a lab partner, but first predict where the ball must hit on the wall to bounce in the right direction. If your partner moves closer (or farther) from the wall, does your rule still work?

Compare and Contrast

Write a general rule that seems to work. Does your rule for the bouncing ball work for predicting the path of light? How is it similar?

_____

_____

_____

_____

_____

_____

_____

_____

_____

_____

Date _____ Period _____ Name _____

Refraction

Place a small hexagonal nut in the center of the bottom of a 1000-mL beaker. Pour water into the beaker until it is half full of water. Look through the sides of the beaker at the nut while placing a ruler along the tabletop so that the edge of the ruler appears to point to the center of the nut. Do you think that the ruler really points to the nut? Look from the top to see where the ruler points. Place a golf ball on the nut. Look through the sides of the beaker at the ball and adjust the edge of the ruler to point to the edge of the ball. Look from the top.

Analyze and Conclude

Describe your observations. Make a drawing to show why the ball appears to be so wide.

_____

_____

_____

_____

_____

_____

Date _____ Period _____ Name _____

17-3

Cool Images

CAUTION: *Avoid staring directly into the laser beam or at bright reflections.*

Can you light an electric bulb without any electrical connection and can you make the image of the bulb in a mirror glow? Try this activity to find out. Place a 100-watt bulb in an electric socket but do not turn on the electricity. Place this next to a mirror. Sit so that you can see both the bulb and its reflection. Aim a penlight laser at the bulb.

Observe and Infer

Did you notice that the bulb glowed red and that the image also glowed? What would happen if you aimed the laser at the image? Try it. Use a ray diagram to explain your results.

_____

_____

_____

_____

_____

Date _____ Period _____ Name _____

17-4

Pocket Lab

Personal Rainbow

You can make your own personal rainbow when the sun is out and low in the sky for easier viewing. Adjust a garden hose to produce a gentle spray. Face away from the sun so that you can see your shadow. Spray the water upwards above your shadow and watch closely until you see the colors. By moving the spray in an arc from side to side, you will produce your own personal rainbow.

Analyze and Conclude

Did you notice the order of the colors in the spectrum of visible lights? Could you easily see each of the colors ROYGBIV? Which color was on the inside edge? Which color was on the outside edge?

_____

_____

_____

_____

_____

_____

_____

_____

_____

_____

18 〰 Physics Lab

Seeing Is Believing

Problem
How can you locate the image of a lens?

Copyright © by Glencoe/McGraw-Hill

Materials

large-diameter convex lens

large-diameter concave lens

2 small balls of clay

2 rulers

2- or 3-cm-long nail

2 pieces of paper

Procedure
1. Assemble the equipment as shown in your text on p. 433 using the concave lens.
2. Look through the lens to make sure that you can see both ends of the nail. Move the nail closer or farther from the lens until both ends are visible.

Data and Observations
1. Mark the paper to show the tip of the nail, the head of the nail, and also the lens line.
2. Line up your straight edge to point to the head of the nail. Have your lab partner verify that the edge is accurate.
3. Draw the line of sight.
4. Move to another position and draw a second line of sight to the head of the nail.
5. Repeat steps 2–4, this time drawing two lines of sight to the tip of the nail.
6. Use a new sheet of paper and repeat steps 1–5 using the convex lens.
7. When you are finished, put away any materials that can be reused.

Analyze And Conclude
1. **Analyzing Data** The image position can be located by extending lines of sight until they intersect. Extend the two lines of sight that point to the image head. Extend the two lines of sight that point to the image tip. Describe the results.

_____

_____

_____

_____

18 Physics Lab

2. Analyzing Data Repeat the analysis for the convex lens, and describe the results.

_____

_____

_____

3. Comparing Data Record your observations and image descriptions in a table.

Table 1			
Lens	**Image Size (with respect to object)**	**Image Type (upright or upside down)**	**Image Location (with respect to object and lens)**
concave			
convex			

4. Extending Results How would the image size and location change if you moved the object closer to the lens? Do the answers depend on whether the lens is concave or convex?

_____

_____

_____

_____

Apply

1. Describe an application of a similar arrangement for a convex lens.

_____

_____

_____

_____

18-1

Pocket Lab

Where's the image?

Suppose that you are standing directly in front of a mirror and see your image. Exactly where is the image? Here is a way to find out. Find a camera with a focusing ring that has distances marked on it. Stand 1.0 m from a mirror and focus on the edge of the mirror. Check the reading on the focusing ring. It should be 1.0 m. Now focus on your image. What is the reading on the ring now?

Analyze and Conclude

Summarize your results and write a brief conclusion.

_____

_____

_____

_____

_____

_____

_____

_____

_____

_____

Date _____ Period _____ Name _____

Real or Virtual?

Hold a small concave mirror at arm's length and look at your image. What do you see? Is the image in front or behind the mirror? What happens to the image as you slowly bring the mirror toward your face?

Analyze and Conclude

Briefly summarize your observations and conclusions.

_____

_____

_____

_____

_____

_____

_____

_____

_____

_____

_____

Physics: Principles and Problems

18-3  Pocket Lab

Focal Points

Take a concave mirror into an area of direct sunlight. Use a piece of clay to hold the mirror steady so that the concave mirror directly faces the sun. Move your finger toward or away from the mirror in the area of reflected light to find the brightest spot (focal point). Turn the mirror so that the convex side faces the sun and repeat the experiment.

Analyze and Conclude

Record and explain your results.

_____

_____

_____

_____

_____

_____

_____

_____

_____

_____

_____

_____

_____

18-4

 Pocket Lab

Makeup

Do you have a makeup mirror in your home? Does this mirror produce images that are larger or smaller than your face? What does this tell you about the curvature? Feel the surface of the mirror. Does this confirm your prediction about the curvature? Try to discover the focal length of this mirror.

Analyze and Conclude

Record your procedure and briefly explain your observations and results.

_____

_____

_____

_____

_____

_____

_____

_____

_____

_____

_____

18-5

Burned Up

Convex (converging) lenses can be used as magnifying glasses. Use someone's eyeglasses to see if they magnify. Are the glasses converging? Can the lenses be used in sunlight to start a fire?

Analyze and Conclude

Use your answers to describe the lenses.

_____

_____

_____

_____

_____

_____

18-6

Fish-Eye Lens

How can fish focus light with their eyes? The light from an object in the water goes from the water into the fish eye, which is also mostly water. Obtain a converging lens and observe that it can be used as a magnifying glass. Now hold the lens under water in an aquarium. Does the lens still magnify?

Analyze and Conclude

Compare the magnifying ability of the glass lens when used under water and in air. Would a more curved lens bend the light more? Would you predict that the index of refraction of the material in a fish eye is the same as water? Defend your prediction.

_____

_____

_____

_____

_____

_____

_____

_____

_____

_____

_____

18-7

Bright Ideas

Stick the edge of a converging lens into a ball of clay and place the lens on a tabletop. Use a small light-bulb on one side and a screen on the other side to get a sharp image of the bulb. Predict what will happen to the image if you place your hand over the top half of the lens. Try it.

Analyze and Conclude

What happened? How much of the lens is needed for a complete image?

_____

_____

_____

_____

_____

_____

_____

19 〰〰 Physics Lab

Wavelengths of Colors

Problem

How can you accurately measure the wavelength of four colors of light?

Materials

meterstick

index card

40-W straight filament light

ball of clay

tape

diffraction grating

Procedure

1. Cut the index card lengthwise into four equal strips.

2. Write the letters "O" (orange), "Y" (yellow), "G" (green), and "B" (blue) on the strips.

3. Place the ball of clay 1.0 m on the bench in front of the lamp. Use the ball of clay to support the diffraction grating.

4. Plug in the lamp and turn off the room lights.

5. When you look through the diffraction grating, you should see bands of colors to the sides of the bulb. If you do not see the colors to the sides, then rotate the diffraction grating 90° until you do.

6. Have a lab partner stand behind the lamp and move the strip labeled "O" from side to side until you see it in place with the middle of its color. Ask your partner to tape the strip to the table at that point.

7. Repeat step 6 for each of the other colored strips.

8. When you are completely finished with the lab, dispose or recycle appropriate materials. Put away materials that can be reused.

Data and Observations

Table 1				
Color	x	d	L	λ

19 Physics Lab

Analyze and Conclude

1. **Observing and Inferring** What color is closest to the lamp? Suggest a reason and list the order that colors occur, beginning from red.

   _____

   _____

   _____

   _____

   _____

2. **Making and Using a Table** Use a data table or a spreadsheet to record x, d, and L for each of the four colors. Measure and record x for each strip to the nearest 0.1 cm. Record the value of d provided by your teacher.

3. **Calculating** Use the equation $\lambda = xd/L$ to calculate the wavelength for each color and record this value in nanometers in your data table or spreadsheet.

Apply

1. How could diffraction gratings be used in conjunction with telescopes?

   _____

   _____

   _____

   _____

   _____

2. Suppose your diffraction grating had more grooves per centimeter. How would this change the diffraction pattern you see?

   _____

   _____

   _____

19-1

Pocket Lab

Hot Lights

Plug a 100-W clear lamp into a Variac (variable power supply). Turn off the room lights. Look through a diffraction grating at the lamp as you slowly increase the power.

Observing and Inferring

Describe what you see. Which color appears first? What happens to the brightness of previous colors as new colors become visible? What is the order of the colors?

_____

_____

_____

_____

_____

_____

_____

_____

_____

_____

_____

_____

19-2

Laser Spots

Turn on a laser so that it makes a spot on the center of a movie screen. What would you expect to happen to the spot if you were to put a piece of window screening in the pathway of the beam? Explain your prediction.

Observing and Interpreting

What really happened? Use the wave theory to explain your results.

_____

_____

_____

_____

_____

_____

_____

_____

_____

_____

_____

Date _____ Period _____ Name _____

19-3

Pocket Lab

Lights in the Night

Obtain small pieces of red and blue cellophane. When it is dark, find a long stretch of road and estimate the distance to cars when you can just barely tell that they have two headlights on. When a car is far away, its lights blend together. Look at these distant lights through the red cellophane and also through the blue cellophane. Which color makes it easier to resolve the two lights into separate images?

Determining Cause and Effect

Explain why one color is more effective in separating the lights. Suggest how the use of blue filters might be useful for scientists working with telescopes or microscopes.

_____

_____

_____

_____

_____

_____

_____

_____

_____

20 〰 Physics Lab

What's the charge?

Problem

Can you see the effects of electrostatic charging? How can you increase the amount of charge on an object without discharging it?

Procedure

1. Paint the pith ball with graphite and allow it to dry.

2. Tape the inverted cup to the aluminum pie pan. Secure the straw to the top of the cup and use the thread to attach the ball as shown in your textbook on page 467.

3. Rub the foam with wool, then remove the wool.

4. Holding onto the plastic cup, lower the pie pan until it is about 3 cm above the foam block and then slowly lift it away.

5. Place the pie pan directly on the charged foam block and lift it away.

6. Bring your finger near the ball until they touch.

7. Place the pie pan on the foam block and touch the edge of the pie pan with your finger. Then remove the pie pan from the foam block and touch the ball again with your finger.

8. Repeat step 7 several times without recharging the foam block.

9. When finished, recycle or dispose of appropriate materials. Put away materials that can be reused.

Materials

30 cm × 30 cm
    block of polystyrene

22-cm aluminum pie pan

plastic cup

drinking straw

wool

transparent tape

thread

pith ball (or small piece
    of plastic foam packing
    material)

liquid graphite

Data and Observations

Table 1	
Description of Event	**Observations**

Name _____

20 Physics Lab

Analyze and Conclude

1. **Forming a Description** As the pie pan was brought near the charged block, could you detect a force between the neutral pie pan and the charged foam block? Describe it.

_____
_____
_____

2. **Interpreting Observations** Explain what happened to the ball in step 4 and step 5.

_____
_____
_____

3. **Analyzing Results** Make a drawing to show the distribution of charges on the neutral pie pan as it is lowered toward the charged foam block.

4. **Inferring Relationships** What was the reason for using the ball on a thread? Explain the back-and-forth motion of the ball in step 6.

_____
_____
_____

5. **Interpreting Observations** Does the polystyrene block seem to run out of charges in step 8?

_____
_____

Apply

1. Clear plastic wrap is sold to seal up containers of food. Suggest a reason why it clings to itself.

_____
_____
_____

Physics: Principles and Problems

20-1  Pocket Lab

Charged Up

Rub a balloon with wool. Touch the balloon to the knob of an electroscope and watch the leaves.

Analyze and Conclude

Describe the result. Make a drawing to explain the result. Touch the knob of the electroscope to make the leaves fall. Would you expect that the wool could move the leaves? Why? Try it. Explain your results.

_____

_____

_____

_____

_____

_____

_____

_____

_____

Date _____ Period _____ Name _____

20-2

Reach Out

Start with the leaves of an electroscope down. Predict what should happen if you bring a charged balloon near (but not touching) the top of the electroscope.

Analyze and Conclude

Explain your prediction. Try it. Describe and explain your results.

_____

_____

_____

_____

_____

_____

_____

_____

_____

Physics: Principles and Problems

21 〰〰 Physics Lab

Charges, Energy, and Voltage

Problem

How can you make a model that demonstrates the relationship of charge, energy, and voltage?

Materials

ball of clay

ruler

cellophane tape

12 steel balls, 3-mm
    diameter

paper

Procedure

1. Use the clay to support the ruler vertically on the tabletop. The 0 end should be at the table.

2. Cut a 2 cm × 8 cm rectangular piece of paper and write on it "3 V = 3 J/C."

3. Cut three more rectangles and label them: 6 V = 6 J/C, 9 V = 9 J/C, and 12 V = 12 J/C.

4. Tape the 3-V rectangle to the 3" mark on the ruler, the 6-V to the 6" mark, and so on.

5. Let each steel ball represent 1 C of charge.

6. Lift and tape four steel balls to the 3-V rectangle, three to the 6-V rectangle, and so on.

7. When you are completely finished with the lab, dispose of or recycle appropriate materials. Put away materials that can be reused.

Data and Observations

1. Review the data table below.

Table 1			
Level	**Charge**	**Voltage**	**Energy**

2. Fill in the data table for your model for each level of the model.

3. The model shows different amounts of charges at different energy levels. Where should steel balls be placed to show a zero energy level? Explain.

_____

_____

21 Physics Lab

Name _____

Analyze and Conclude

1. **Analyzing Data** How much energy is required to lift each coulomb of charge from the tabletop to the 9-V level?

_____

_____

_____

2. **Analyzing Data** What is the total potential energy stored in the 9-V level?

_____

_____

_____

3. **Relating Concepts** The total energy of the charges in the 6-V level is not 6 J. Explain this.

_____

_____

_____

_____

_____

4. **Making Predictions** How much energy would be given off if the charges in the 9-V level fell to the 6-V level? Explain.

_____

_____

_____

_____

Apply

1. A 9-V battery is very small. A 12-V car battery is very big. Use your model to help explain why two 9-V batteries will not start your car.

_____

_____

_____

_____

_____

_____

 Pocket Lab

Electric Fields

How does the electric field around a charged piece of plastic foam vary in strength and direction? Try this activity to find out. Tie a pith ball on the end of a 20-cm nylon thread and tie the other end to a plastic straw. When you hold the straw horizontally, notice that the ball hangs straight down on the thread. Now rub a piece of wool on a 30 cm × 30 cm square of plastic foam to charge both objects. Stand the foam in a vertical orientation. Hold the straw and touch the pith ball to the wool, then slowly bring the hanging ball towards the charged plastic foam. Move the pith ball to different regions and notice the angle of the thread.

Analyze and Conclude

Why did the ball swing toward the charged plastic? Explain in terms of the electric field. Did the angle of the thread change? Why? Does the angle of the thread indicate the direction of the electric field? Explain.

_____

_____

_____

_____

_____

_____

_____

_____

_____

22 ⟁⟁⟁ Physics Lab

Mystery Cans

Problem

An electric device is inside each film can. How can you design and build a circuit to determine whether the resistance is constant for different voltages?

Materials

power supply with
   variable voltage

wires with clips

multimeter

ammeter

3 film cans for each group

Procedure

1. Identify the variables to be measured.

2. Design your circuit and label each component. Use the proper symbols to make your drawing of the setup. Show your teacher your plan before proceeding further.

3. Build the circuit of your design and slowly increase the voltage on your power supply to make sure that your meters are working properly. Do not exceed one amp or the current limitation set by your teacher. Reverse connections as needed.

4. Make at least three measurements of voltage and current for each can.

5. When you have completed the lab, put away materials that can be reused. Dispose of or recycle materials as appropriate.

Data and Observations

1. Make a data table with at least three places for measurements on each can.

Table 1				
	Trial	V	I	R
Can 1				
Can 2				
Can 3				

22 Physics Lab

Analyze and Conclude

1. **Calculating Results** Calculate R for each test.

2. **Graphing Data** Graph V versus I for all of your data. If possible, use a graphing calculator or computer plotting program. Draw a separate line for each can. Identify the relationship between variables.

3. **Interpreting Graphs** Determine the slope for each of your lines.

4. **Comparing Values** Open each can to see the marked values of the resistors. Compare your predicted values to the actual values.

_____
_____
_____
_____
_____
_____
_____

22 Physics Lab

Apply

1. Most incandescent lamps burn out when they are switched on rather than when they have been on for a while. Predict what happens to the resistance and the current when a cold lamp is switched on. Make a graph of R versus t and also I versus t for the first few seconds. Calculate the resistance of an operating 60-W lamp at 120 V. Now use a multimeter as an ohmmeter to measure the resistance of a cold 60-W lamp. Describe your results.

_____

_____

_____

_____

_____

Date _____   Period _____   Name _____

22-1

Lighting Up

Use a D cell and a 10-cm length of wire to light a miniature lamp. Make a sketch of two circuits that work and two circuits that do not work.

Analyze and Conclude

Can you light the lamp without having two connecting points on the lamp? Does a lamp connected in your house have two connecting points? Suggest a reason why two are needed.

_____

_____

_____

_____

_____

_____

_____

_____

22-2

Pocket Lab

Running Out

Use the proper symbols and design a drawing that shows a power supply in a continuous circuit with two miniature lamps. Next, draw the circuit with an ammeter included to measure the electrical flow between the power supply and the bulbs. Make a third drawing to show the ammeter at a position to measure the electrical flow between the bulbs.

Test Your Prediction

Would you predict the current between the lamps to be more or less than the current before the lamps? Why? Build the circuits to find out. Record your results.

_____

_____

_____

_____

_____

_____

_____

_____

22-3

Appliances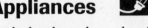

Look closely at three electric appliances in your home. Record the power (watts) or the current (amps) of each appliance. Assume that each appliance operates at 120 V. Determine the resistance of each appliance.

Analyze and Conclude

Relate the power used in an appliance to its resistance.

_____

_____

_____

_____

_____

_____

_____

22-4

Pocket Lab

Heating Up

Look at the markings on three resistors. Predict which resistor would allow the most current through it using a constant voltage. Under the same conditions, predict which resistor will heat the most. Explain your prediction.

_____

_____

_____

_____

_____

_____

Test Your Predictions

Tape a thermometer bulb to the resistor. Turn on the power for one minute. Measure the temperature. Allow the resistor to cool off and then repeat the procedure with the remaining two resistors.

CAUTION: *Do not touch the resistors with power supplied. They may be extremely hot. Wait two minutes after turning off the power to remove the thermometer.*

23 ‿‿‿ Design Your Own Physics Lab

Circuits

Problem

Suppose that three identical lamps are connected to the same power supply. Can a circuit be made such that one lamp is brighter than the others and stays on if either of the others is loosened in its socket?

Hypothesis

One lamp should be brighter than the other two and remain at the same brightness when either of the other two lamps is loosened in its socket so that it goes out.

Plan the Experiment

1. Sketch a series circuit and predict the relative brightness of each lamp. Predict what would happen to the other lamps when one is loosened so that it goes out.

2. Sketch a parallel circuit and predict the relative brightness of each lamp. Predict what would happen to the other lamps when one is loosened so that it goes out.

3. Draw a combination circuit. Label the lamps A, B, and C. Would the bulbs have the same brightness? Predict what would happen to the other two lamps when each lamp in turn is loosened so that it goes out.

4. **Check the Plan** Show your circuits and predictions to your teacher before starting to build the circuits.

5. When you have completed the lab, dispose of or recycle appropriate materials. Put away materials that can be reused.

Analyze and Conclude

1. **Interpreting Data** Did the series circuit meet the requirements? Explain.

_____

_____

_____

2. **Interpreting Data** Did the parallel circuit meet either of the requirements? Explain.

_____

_____

_____

Possible Materials

power supply with
    variable voltage

wires with clips

3 identical lamps and
    sockets

23 Physics Lab

3. **Formulating Hypotheses** Explain the circuit that solved the problem in terms of current.

_____

_____

_____

_____

4. **Formulating Hypotheses** Use the definition of *resistance* to explain why one lamp was brighter and the other two were equally dim.

_____

_____

_____

5. **Making Predictions** Predict how the voltages would compare when measured across each lamp in the correct circuit.

_____

_____

_____

6. **Testing Conclusions** Use a voltmeter to check your prediction.

Apply

1. Can one wall switch control several lights in the same room? Are the lamps in parallel or series? Are the switches in parallel or series with the lamps? Explain.

_____

_____

_____

_____

23-1

Series Resistance

Hook up a power supply, a resistor, and an ammeter in a series circuit. Predict what will happen to the current in the circuit when a second, identical resistor is added in series to the circuit. Predict the new currents when the circuit contains three and four resistors in series. Explain your prediction. Try it.

_____

_____

_____

_____

_____

Analyze and Conclude

Make a data table to show your results. Briefly explain your results. (**Hint:** Include the idea of resistance.)

_____

_____

_____

_____

_____

23-2

Parallel Resistance

Hook up a power supply, a resistor, and an ammeter in a series circuit. Predict what will happen to the current in the circuit when a second, identical resistor is added in parallel to the first. Predict the new currents when the circuit contains three and four resistors in parallel. Explain your prediction. Try it.

_____

_____

_____

_____

_____

Analyze and Conclude

Make a data table to show your results. Briefly explain your results. (**Hint:** Include the idea of resistance.)

_____

_____

_____

_____

_____

23-3 Pocket Lab

Ammeter Resistance

Design an experiment using a power supply, a voltmeter, an ammeter, a resistor, and some wires to determine the resistance of the ammeter. Make a sketch of your setup and include measurements and equations.

Communicating Results

What is the resistance of the ammeter? Be prepared to present your experiment to the class.

_____

_____

_____

_____

24 〜 Design Your Own
Physics Lab

Coils and Currents

Problem

You have seen that an electric current affects a magnetic compass needle. What happens to pieces of iron located inside a coil that carries a current? What is the effect of changing the magnitude of the current? Does an alternating current produce a different effect from that of a direct current?

Hypothesis

Write a testable hypothesis that addresses the questions posed in the problem.

_____

_____

_____

_____

_____

_____

Possible Materials

a ring stand with crossbar and clamp

two 20-cm lengths of thick, insulated iron wire

75 cm of thread

magnetic compass

miniature lamp with socket

500-turn, aircore solenoid

a variable power supply that can produce AC and DC voltages and currents

electrical leads and alligator clips

Plan the Experiment

1. Develop a plan and design a circuit you can use to test your hypothesis.

2. **Check the Plan** Show your teacher your plan before you start to build the circuit. **CAUTION:** *Be sure the power supply is off as you build the circuit.*

3. **CAUTION:** *Your teacher must inspect your setup before you turn the power on and begin your investigation.*

4. When you have completed the lab, dispose of or recycle appropriate materials. Put away materials that can be reused.

Analyze and Conclude

1. **Making Observations** Describe your observations as you increased the direct current produced by the power supply.

_____

_____

_____

_____

24 Physics Lab

2. Drawing Conclusions What conclusion can you make regarding the strength of the magnetic field as you increased the current?

_____

_____

_____

3. Interpreting Results What can you conclude from the results of your experimentation comparing the effects of direct and alternating currents?

_____

_____

_____

_____

4. Making Predictions Predict what would happen to the magnetic field if the number of turns on the coil was doubled. How would you test your prediction?

_____

_____

_____

_____

_____

Apply

1. Large and powerful electromagnets are often used at scrap metal facilities. Would you expect that these magnets use AC current or DC current? Explain why.

_____

_____

_____

_____

2. In some apartment and office buildings, a tenant can "buzz" visitors into the building using a switch inside his or her unit. Explain how coils and currents work together to make this possible.

_____

_____

_____

_____

24-1

Monopoles?

Place a disk magnet flat on the center of your paper. Place another disk magnet flat at the top of your paper and slowly slide it toward the center magnet.

Observing and Inferring

Does the first magnet attract or repel the second magnet? Rotate one of the magnets and note the effect on the other. Does each magnet have only one pole?

_____

_____

_____

_____

_____

_____

_____

24-2

Funny Balls 👓

Place a disk magnet flat on your paper. Roll a 3-mm steel ball at the magnet. Place a second steel ball on the paper, touching the magnet and the first steel ball.

Hypothesizing

What happens? Why? Make a sketch to help explain your hypothesis. Devise a procedure to test your hypothesis.

_____

_____

_____

_____

_____

_____

_____

_____

_____

_____

_____

_____

24-3 Pocket Lab

3-D Magnetic Fields

Most illustrations are able to show the shape of the magnetic field around a magnet only two-dimensionally. Try this activity to see the shape of a magnetic field in 3-D. Tie a string to the middle of a nail so that the nail will hang horizontally. Put a small piece of tape around the string where it wraps around the nail so that the string will not slip. Insert the nail into a coil and apply a voltage to the coil. This will magnetize the nail. Turn off the power to the coil and remove the nail. Now hold the string to suspend the nail and slowly move it close to a permanent magnet. Try this for magnets of various shapes.

Analyze

What evidence do you have that the nail became magnetized? Using your results, make a 3-D drawing that shows the magnetic field around the nail.

_____

_____

_____

_____

_____

_____

25 〰️ Design Your Own
Physics Lab

Swinging Coils

Problem

Electricity that you use in your everyday life comes from the wall socket or from chemical batteries. Modern theory suggests that current can be caused by the interactions of wires and magnets. Exactly how do coils and magnets interact?

Hypothesis

Form a testable hypothesis that relates to the interaction of magnets and coils. Be sure to include some symmetry tests in your hypothesis. Try to design a system of coils and magnets so that you can use one pair as a generator and one pair as a motor.

_____

_____

_____

Possible Materials

coils of enameled wire

identical sets of magnets

masking tape

supports and bars

Plan the Experiment

1. Devise a means to test stationary effects: those that occur when the magnet and coils are not moving.

2. Consider how to test moving effects: those that occur when the magnet moves in various directions in relation to the coil.

3. Include different combinations of connecting, or not connecting, the ends of the wires.

4. Consider polarity, magnetic strength, and any other variables that might influence the interaction of the coils and magnet.

5. **Check the Plan** Make sure that your teacher has approved your final plan before you proceed with your experiment.

6. When you have completed the lab, dispose of or recycle appropriate materials. Put away materials that can be reused.

Analyze and Conclude

1. **Organizing Results** Construct a list of tests that you performed and their results.

_____

_____

_____

_____

25 Physics Lab

2. Analyzing Data Summarize the effects of the stationary magnet and the moving magnet. Explain how connecting the wires influenced your results.

_____

_____

_____

_____

_____

_____

3. Relating Concepts Describe and explain the effects of changing polarity, direction, number of coils, and any other variables you used.

_____

_____

_____

_____

_____

4. Checking Your Hypothesis Did the experiment yield expected results? Did you determine any new interactions?

_____

_____

_____

Apply

1. The current that you generated in this activity was quite small. List several factors that you could change to generate more current. (**Hint:** Think of a commercial generator.)

_____

_____

_____

_____

_____

25-1 Pocket Lab

Making Currents

Hook the ends of a 1-m length of wire to the binding posts of a galvanometer (or microammeter). Make several overlapping loops in the wire. Watch the readings on the wire as you move a pair of neodymium magnets (or a strong horseshoe magnet) near the loops. Record your observations.

Analyze and Conclude

What can you do to increase the current? Replace the 1-m length of wire with a preformed coil and see how much current you can produce. Describe your results.

_____

_____

_____

_____

_____

_____

_____

_____

_____

_____

25-2

Motor and Generator

Make a series circuit with a Genecon (or efficient DC motor), a miniature lamp, and an ammeter. Rotate the handle (or motor shaft) to try to light the lamp.

Analyze and Conclude

Describe your results. Predict what might happen if you connect your Genecon to the Genecon from another lab group and crank yours. Try it. Describe what happens. Can more than two be connected?

_____

_____

_____

_____

_____

_____

_____

_____

_____

_____

_____

_____

_____

Slow Motor

Make a series circuit with a miniature DC motor, an ammeter, and a DC power supply. Hook up a voltmeter in parallel across the motor. Adjust the setting on the power supply so that the motor is running at medium speed. Make a data table to show the readings on the ammeter and voltmeter.

Analyze and Conclude

Predict what will happen to the readings on the circuit when you hold the shaft and keep it from turning. Try it. Explain the results.

_____

_____

_____

_____

_____

_____

_____

_____

_____

_____

_____

_____

25-4

Slow Magnet

Lay a 1-m length of copper tube on the lab table. Try to pull the copper with a pair of neodymium magnets. Can you feel any force on the copper? Hold the tube by one end so that it hangs straight down. Drop a small steel marble through the tube. Use a stopwatch to measure the time needed for first the marble and then for the pair of magnets to fall through the tube. Catch the magnets in your hand. If they hit the table or floor, they will break.

Analyze and Conclude

Devise a hypothesis that would explain the strange behavior of the falling magnets and suggest a method of testing your hypothesis.

_____

_____

_____

_____

_____

_____

_____

_____

_____

_____

_____

26 ⋙ Physics Lab

Simulating a Mass Spectrometer

Problem

How can you simulate the working parts of a mass spectrometer?

Procedure

1. Build the apparatus as shown in the diagram on page 612 of your textbook. Place a ball of clay under one side of the wave tank so that the tank is slightly sloped.

2. Make a test trial, allowing the steel ball to roll down the track. The ball should follow a curved path similar to the one shown in the diagram when it is started halfway up the ruler.

3. Starting from the same spot on the ruler, roll the steel ball down the track three times. Mark the positions where the ball crosses the far side of the graph paper.

4. Place the permanent magnets on the paper so they pull the ball slightly toward the high end of the slope. Adjust the magnets so that the ball follows a straight path across the graph paper, as shown in the diagram.

5. Releasing the ball from the same spot on the ruler, repeat step 3.

6. When you have completed the lab, dispose of or recycle appropriate materials. Put away materials that can be reused.

Materials

🥽 🧤

2 balls of clay

grooved ruler

6-mm steel ball

glass marble

graph paper

masking tape

2 permanent magnets

cafeteria tray or glass wave tank

Data and Observations

1. Describe the path of the ball in step 3.

_____

_____

_____

_____

2. Describe the path of the ball in step 5.

_____

_____

_____

_____

26 Physics Lab

Analyze and Conclude

1. Thinking Critically In this model, you used gravity to simulate the electric field of a mass spectrometer. How could the electric field in this model be varied?

_____

_____

_____

_____

_____

2. Analyzing Data What happens to the path as the magnet is brought closer to the path of the ball? Why?

_____

_____

_____

_____

_____

3. Thinking Critically If you release the ball from a higher location, the ball will leave the ruler with more speed. In this case, the path will curve less, even though the force on the ball is the same. Why?

_____

Apply

1. Predict what would happen to a 6-mm ball that had the same mass, but less or no iron content. Explain your prediction. Test it.

_____

_____

_____

_____

_____

_____

_____

26-1

Rolling Along

Place a small ball of clay under one end of a grooved ruler to make a ramp. Roll a 6-mm-diameter steel ball down the ramp and along the tabletop. Place a strong magnet near the path of the ball so that the ball will curve, but not hit the magnet. Predict what will happen to the path when the ball is started higher or lower on the ramp. Try it.

Analyze and Conclude

Is this consistent for a charged particle moving through a magnetic field?

_____

_____

_____

_____

_____

_____

26-2

Catching the Wave

When you listen to your radio, you are hearing the information that is carried by electromagnetic waves. Many electronic and electrical devices produce low-frequency electromagnetic waves. Use a telephone pickup coil along with an amplifier to try to pick up signals from such devices as a television, computer, light, burning candle, coffee maker, or vacuum cleaner.

Analyzing Data

Describe and interpret your results.

_____

_____

_____

_____

_____

_____

_____

_____

_____

_____

_____

_____

_____

26-3 Pocket Lab

More Radio Stuff

Radio stations broadcast with tremendous power from tall towers. Would it be possible to make your own radio transmitter and receiver? Try this activity to find out. Pop your favorite tape into a tape player, or tune your portable radio to a strong local AM station. Next, put a miniplug into the earphone jack, and attach the two leads to the ends of an air core solenoid. Put a second miniplug into a mini-amp speaker, and attach the leads to the ends of a second air core solenoid. Turn the power on for the miniamp speaker, and listen for the sound.

Make a Hypothesis

Make a hypothesis explaining why this lab works. Try changing the distance between the solenoids. Explain your results.

_____

_____

_____

_____

_____

_____

_____

_____

_____

_____

_____

_____

27 〰〰 Physics Lab

Red Hot or Not?

Problem

How well do steel balls simulate the photoelectric effect?

Procedure

1. Shape the grooved channel as shown in the diagram in your text-book on page 634. Mark a point on the channel, 4 cm above the table, with R for red.

2. Mark a point on the channel, 14 cm above the table, with V for violet. Place marks for blue, green, yellow, and orange uniformly between R and V.

3. Place two steel balls at the lowest point on the channel. These steel balls represent valence electrons in the atom.

4. Place a steel ball on the channel at the red mark. This represents a photon of red light, which has the lowest energy of the six colors of light being modeled.

5. Release the photon and see if the electrons are removed from the atom; that is, see if either steel ball escapes from the channel.

6. Remove the steel ball that represents the photon from the lower part of the channel.

7. Repeat steps 4–6 for each color's mark on the channel. **Note:** Always start with two electrons at the low point in the channel. Record your observations.

8. When you have completed the lab, dispose of or recycle appropriate materials. Put away materials that can be reused.

Materials

2-cm steel balls

grooved channel
   (U-channel or shelf
   bracket)

red, orange, yellow, green,
   blue, and violet
   marking pens or
   colored stickers

Data and Observations

1. Identify the photons by the color mark from which they were released. Which color of photons was able to remove the electrons?

   _____

   _____

   _____

   _____

2. Did one photon ever remove more than one electron? If so, what was its color?

   _____

   _____

27 Physics Lab

3. Summarize your observations in terms of the energies of the photons.

_____
_____
_____
_____
_____

Analyze and Conclude

1. **Making Predictions** Predict what would happen if two red photons could hit the electrons at the same time.

_____
_____
_____
_____

2. **Testing Predictions** Start two steel balls (photons) at the red mark on the channel and see what happens. Describe the results.

_____
_____
_____

3. **Making Inferences** Some materials hold their valence electrons tighter than others. How could the model be modified to show this?

_____
_____

Apply

1. Photographers often have red lights in their darkrooms. Explain why they use red light but not blue light.

_____
_____
_____

Glows in the Dark

Close the shades and turn off the lights in the room. Shine a flashlight at a beaker that contains fluorescein. Now place a red filter over the flashlight so that only red light hits the beaker. Describe the results. Repeat the experiment using a green filter. Explain the results. Would you expect the fluorescein to glow when a blue filter is used? Explain your prediction. Try it.

Analyze and Conclude

Write a brief explanation of your observations.

_____

_____

_____

_____

_____

_____

_____

_____

27-2

 *Pocket Lab*

See the Light

Close the shades and turn off all the lights in the room. Look at a 150-W lamp as you use a dimmer switch to slowly increase and decrease the voltage across the lamp. Describe what you observe. What would you expect to see if you repeated the experiment while looking through a diffraction grating? Why? Try it. Describe your results.

Analyze and Conclude

Describe your observations.

_____

_____

_____

_____

_____

_____

_____

_____

_____

_____

_____

_____

28 〰️ Physics Lab

Shots in the Dark

Problem

Given that the atom is mostly empty space, how easy is it to hit a nucleus and cause atomic scattering?

Materials

3 dozen rubber stoppers

bedsheet (or blanket)

blindfold (or darkened goggles)

six 9-inch aluminum pie pans

four 1.5-meter 1 × 2 wood pieces

fishing line

Procedure

1. Construct the model according to the diagram in your textbook on page 656.

2. Each student will be blindfolded, led to a position 3 m directly in front of the target area, and allowed to toss ten rubber stoppers (one at a time) into the target area. If a rubber stopper does not strike within the target area, the shooter should be told "too high," "too low," and so on and be given an extra rubber stopper.

3. Students will be able to hear the nuclear "hit" when the rubber stopper hits the target area. Only one hit will be counted on a single target.

4. When you have completed the lab, dispose of or recycle appropriate materials. Put away materials that can be reused.

Data and Observations

Table 1		
Student's Name	Number of Shots	Number of Hits

28 Physics Lab

Name _____

Analyze and Conclude

There are six circular targets within the target area. The ratio of hits to shots is represented by the following:

$$\frac{\text{hits}}{\text{shots}} = \frac{\text{total target area}}{\text{total model area}} = \frac{6\pi r^2}{\text{width} \times \text{height}}$$

1. **Analyzing Data** Use the class totals for shots and hits to calculate the total area for the six targets. Estimate the area for each target. Then calculate the radius for each target.

2. **Relating Concepts** The uncertainty for this experiment decreases with more shots. The percentage uncertainty is represented by the following:

$$\% \text{ uncertainty} = \frac{(\text{shots})^{1/2}}{\text{shots}} \times 100$$

Find the uncertainty for your class.

Apply

1. A recent phone poll sampled 800 people. Estimate the uncertainty in the poll.

Nuclear Bouncing

Place a 9-inch aluminum pie pan on a table. Gently press four glass marbles (protons) into the pie pan so that they sit in small indentations near the center of the pan. Roll a 12-mm steel ball (alpha particle) down a grooved ruler to see if you can hit the marbles. Then remove the marbles and put the steel balls into the indentations (each steel ball represents a nucleus) in the pie pan and roll a marble (alpha particle) down the grooved ruler.

Analyze and Conclude

When you roll the steel ball at the marbles, does it change its path? Does the steel ball ever bounce back? When you switch the balls and marbles, how are the results different? Why are the results different? Hypothesize what will happen when an alpha particle hits a proton.

_____

_____

_____

_____

_____

_____

_____

_____

_____

_____

28-2

Pocket Lab

Bright Lines

Turn on a gas-discharge tube power supply attached to a gas tube so that the tube glows. **CAUTION:** *Do not touch any exposed metal when the power supply is turned on. Dangerous high voltages are present. Always turn off the power supply before changing gas tubes.* Turn off the room lights. Describe the color. Now look through a diffraction grating at the tube.

Analyze and Conclude

Make a sketch of the results. Repeat this activity with a different gas tube. Explain the differences.

_____

_____

_____

_____

_____

_____

28-3

Laser Diffraction

CAUTION: *Avoid staring directly into the laser beam or at bright reflections.* A diffraction grating separates light from discharge tubes into individual wavelengths. Predict what will happen when you shine a laser light through a diffraction grating. Shine the laser at a sheet of white paper about 1 foot away. Then place the diffraction grating next to the laser to see what happens.

Analyze and Conclude

Describe and explain your results. Predict how your results would be similar and different with a green laser light.

_____

_____

_____

_____

_____

_____

_____

_____

_____

_____

29 〰〰 Physics Lab

The Stoplight

Problem

How can you design a circuit so that changing the direction of the current changes the LED that lights up?

Materials

0- to 12-V variable power supply
red LED
green LED
bicolored LED
wires
470-Ω resistor
voltmeter

Procedure

1. Connect a series circuit with the power supply, the resistor, and the red and green LEDs to light them both. Do not bypass or omit the resistor with an LED. Always have the resistor between an LED and one side of the power supply.

2. Reverse the direction of the current in the circuit and note the result. Measure the voltage across an LED.

3. Design a circuit so that changing the direction of the current will change the color that lights up.

4. Test your circuit.

5. When you have completed the lab, dispose of or recycle appropriate materials. Put away materials that can be reused.

Data and Observations

1. What voltage was needed to light the LEDs?

_____

_____

2. Describe what happened when the current was reversed.

_____

_____

_____

Analyze and Conclude

1. **Diagramming a Circuit** Make a drawing to show your stoplight circuit (red on, green off; then green on, red off).

29 Physics Lab

2. **Explaining Results** Why does your stoplight circuit work?

_____

_____

_____

3. **Analyzing Results** Is your circuit a series or parallel circuit?

_____

_____

_____

4. **Making Predictions** What change would you observe if you replaced the resistor with a 330-Ω resistor?

_____

_____

_____

5. **Forming a Hypothesis** If the voltage across the LED was increased, what would happen to the current?

_____

6. **Thinking Critically** What must be true for the graph or current versus voltage to be a straight line?

_____

_____

Apply

1. Design and conduct experiments to discover what type of LED the bicolored LED is. Remember to leave the resistor connected to the power supply.

_____

_____

_____

2. How does an LED differ from a 60-W lightbulb?

_____

_____

_____

_____

Date _____   Period _____   Name _____

29-1

All Aboard!

Metals become better conductors when they are cooled. Semiconductors become better conductors when they are heated. Does a thermistor act like a metal or a semiconductor?

Make a series circuit with a low-voltage DC power supply, a thermistor, and an ammeter (0–100 mA scale). Slowly turn up the power supply until the needle is in the middle of the scale (50 mA). The voltage will be about 0.6 V. Watch what happens to the current when you hold the thermistor between your fingers. Describe the results.

_____

_____

_____

_____

Comparing and Contrasting

List several possible advantages of thermistors over standard thermometers.

_____

_____

_____

_____

_____

_____

_____

_____

_____

Copyright © by Glencoe/McGraw-Hill

Physics: Principles and Problems

Physics Lab and Pocket Lab Worksheets **159**

29-2

Pocket Lab

Red Light

Make a series circuit with a power supply, a 470-Ω resistor, and a red LED. Connect the short lead of the LED to the negative side of the power supply. Attach the other lead to the resistor. Hook the remaining resistor lead to the positive side of the power supply. Slowly increase the voltage until the LED glows. Note the voltage setting on the power supply.

Hypothesize

What will happen if you reverse the direction of current? Why? Try it and explain what happens.

_____

_____

_____

_____

_____

_____

_____

_____

_____

_____

_____

_____

30 〰️ Physics Lab

Heads Up

Problem

How does the activity of radioactive materials decrease over time? Devise a model of the radioactive decay system.

Materials

> 20 pennies
> graph paper

Procedure

1. Set up a data table as shown, or use a spreadsheet. Turn the pennies so that they are all heads. In this simulation, a heads indicates that the nucleus has not decayed.
2. Flip each coin separately and put the heads and tails into separate piles.
3. Record the number of heads on your data sheet or spreadsheet. Remove the pennies that came up tails.
4. Flip all remaining coins and separate the heads and tails. Count the number of heads and record the value.
5. Repeat steps 2–4 one more time.
6. Share your data with four other students and copy their data onto your data sheet or spreadsheet.

Data and Observations

Table 1						
	You	**Other Students**				**Total**
Begin	20	20	20	20	20	100
Trial 1						
Trial 2						
Trial 3						

30 Physics Lab

Analyze and Conclude

1. **Comparing Data** Did each person have the same number of heads after each trial?

   _____

   _____

2. **Analyzing Data** Is the number of heads close to what you expected?

   _____

   _____

3. **Graphing Results** Total the number of heads remaining for each trial. Make a graph of the number of heads (vertical) verses the trial (horizontal). If possible, use a graphing calculator or a computer plotting program.

4. **Interpreting Graphs** Evaluate and compare your results to the theoretical graph shown in the lab on page 700 of your textbook. Propose explanations for any differences you notice.

   _____

   _____

   _____

5. **Understanding Procedures** Explain the rationale for collecting the results from other students and using the sum of all the results for graphing and analysis.

   _____

   _____

Apply

1. Radioactive materials are often used in medicine for diagnostic purposes. Are these radioisotopes likely to have a short or a long half-life? Explain.

   _____

   _____

2. Laws mandate that hospitals keep radioactive materials for 10 half-lives before disposing of them. Calculate the fraction of the original activity left at the end of 10 half-lives.

Pocket Lab

Background Radiation

Place a Geiger counter on the lab table far away from any sources of radiation. Turn the counter on and record the number of counts for a three-minute interval. Tape a piece of paper around the tube to cover the window and repeat the measurements.

Analyze and Conclude

Did the count go down? What type of radiation could the counter be receiving? Explain.

_____

_____

_____

_____

_____

_____

_____

_____

_____

_____

_____

30-2

Follow the Tracks

CAUTION: *Avoid extended contact with a radioactive source. Handle with extreme caution.* Prepare a cloud chamber by soaking the cloth ring in alcohol. Place the radioactive needle into the side of the cloud chamber and then place the chamber on a block of dry ice. After the chamber cools down, you should be able to observe the tracks of the radiation.

Analyze and Conclude

Predict what might happen when you place a small neodymium magnet in the bottom of the center of the chamber. Try it. Describe the results.

_____

_____

_____

_____

_____

_____

_____

_____

_____

_____

_____

_____

31 〰〰 Physics Lab

Solar Power

Problem

How can you measure the local power output from the nearest continuous running fusion reactor, the sun?

Procedure

1. With no load attached, measure the voltage output of a solar cell when the cell is outdoors and directly facing the sun.

2. Measure the current from the solar cell when the cell is outdoors and directly facing the sun.

3. Measure the length and width of the solar cell and determine its surface area.

4. Remeasure the voltage and current when the sunlight passes through a window.

Data and Observations

Materials

solar cell
voltmeter
ammeter
electrical leads
ruler

Table 1			
Voltage Indoor	Voltage Outdoor	Current Indoor	Current Outdoor

31 Physics Lab

Analyze and Conclude

1. **Calculating Results** Calculate the power, *IV*, for the solar cell outdoors and indoors. What percentage of power did the window stop?

2. **Calculating Results** Calculate the amount of power that could be produced by a cell that has an area of 1.0 square meter.

3. **Calculating Efficiency** The sun supplies about 1000 W of power per square meter to Earth. Calculate the efficiency of your solar cell.

Apply

1. You are planning to install 15 square meters of solar cells on your roof. How much power will you expect them to produce?

   _____

   _____

   _____

   _____

2. Solar panels are used to power satellites in orbit. These panels are generally more efficient than those used on Earth. Why, then, do the satellites still carry batteries?

   _____

   _____

   _____

31-1

Binding Energy

Particles within the nucleus are strongly bonded. Place two disk magnets together to represent a proton and neutron within a nucleus. Slowly pull them apart. Feel how the force changes with separation.

Analyze and Conclude

Describe how this analogy could be extended for a nucleus that contains several protons and neutrons.

_____

_____

_____

_____

_____

_____

_____

_____

_____

_____

_____

31-2  Pocket Lab

Power Plant

Call your local electric company and ask the following questions.

1. Where is the nearest nuclear power plant?

_____

2. What fraction (or percentage) of electricity is supplied by nuclear power in your area?

_____

Analyze and Conclude

How much electrical energy in your neighborhood is provided by nuclear power and how much is provided by other sources?

_____

_____

_____

_____

_____

_____

_____

_____

_____

1 〰 Physics Lab

Egg Drop Project

Problem

Instruments destined to explore Mars or the moon must be packaged so that they are not damaged upon takeoff or landing. You and your partners will create a model for that package. You will design a container for an egg that will keep the egg from breaking when dropped from a height of approximately 5 m.

Possible Materials

cushioning materials such as cotton balls, bubble wrap, balloons, and so on

tape, glue

raw egg

pan balance

3-m × 3-m square plastic drop cloth

paper towels and trash bags

Procedure

1. Work with your group to think of several container designs that might protect an egg. Follow the restrictions below.
   - The design must allow easy opening and closing for egg inspection.
   - Before the container is dropped, it must fit into a 25-cm × 25-cm × 25-cm cube.
   - No liquids are allowed.
   - The egg must be raw, its shell uncoated.
   - The egg must survive a drop from approximately 5 m.
   - Designs with lower mass receive higher scores.

2. Decide which aspects of each idea should be incorporated into your final design.

3. Plan ahead. Set a timetable for experimentation, construction, testing, and redesigning if needed.

4. Make a list of materials you would like to use for your package.

5. Produce a detailed diagram or illustration of your container. Indicate which features you expect will contribute directly to the saftey of the egg.

6. Plan for a test drop of a few centimeters. If your egg breaks, revise your design. If you are satisfied with your design, continue.

7. Record the mass of your container (including egg).

8. Complete the actual egg drop. Inspect your egg. Give your container 10 points if the egg is unbroken, 5 points if the shell is cracked, $\frac{1}{2}$ point if the egg is broken. Find your score using the information below.

$$\text{Score} = \frac{2000}{\text{mass of container}} \times \text{earned egg points}$$

9. Dispose of the egg and materials with egg on them as instructed by your teacher. Clean and put away materials that can be reused.

---

1 Physics Lab

Analyze and Conclude

1. **Compare and Contrast** Which restriction did your team feel was the most limiting? **Students' responses will vary. Many students will find the opening and closing restriction the most troublesome.**

2. **Analyzing the Results** What was the most effective part of your design? What was the weakest part? **Some students will have difficulty isolating parts of the design and determining which part was effective and which was not.**

Apply

1. How would your container need to be redesigned so that it could safely carry two raw eggs? **Students will most likely pair two containers, an egg in each, rather than redesigning their container so it can accommodate two eggs.**

Data and Observations

Table 1

Group	Design	Container Mass	Score

1-1 Pocket Lab

Falling

The Greek philosophers argued that heavy objects fall faster than light objects. Galileo stated that light and heavy objects fall at the same rate. What do you think? Drop four pennies taped together and a single penny from the same height at the same time. Tear a sheet of paper in half. Crumple one piece into a ball. Repeat your experiment with the paper ball and the half sheet of paper. What did you observe each time?

Analyze and Conclude

Who was correct, the Greeks or Galileo?

The Greeks, hence Aristotle, were wrong. If they were correct, the four pennies would have fallen

faster than the single penny and reached the ground first.

---

2 Design Your Own Physics Lab

Mystery Plot

Problem

Can you accurately predict the unknown mass of an object by making measurements of other similar objects?

Hypothesis

Form a hypothesis that relates the mass of an object to another measurable quantity. Describe the variables to be measured and why these measurements are necessary.

Students may hypothesize that the mass of an object can be

determined if the masses of similar objects are known.

Possible Materials

4 pieces of electrical wire with lengths between 5 cm and 30 cm

3 rectangular pieces of floor tile

1 triangular piece of floor tile

metric ruler

balance

graph paper

Plan the Experiment

1. As a group, examine the pieces of floor tile and the pieces of electrical wire. Determine the quantities you want to measure. How can you assure the accuracy and precision of your measurements?

2. Identify the independent and dependent variables.

3. Which objects will be the unknown objects? Which objects will be measured? Set aside the unknowns.

4. Construct a data table or spreadsheet that will include all your measurements and calculations.

5. **Check the Plan** Make sure your teacher has approved your final plan before you proceed with your experiment.

6. Recycle and put away materials that can be reused when you are finished.

Analyze and Conclude

1. **Graphing Data** Make graphs of your measurements to observe relationships between variables. Clearly label the axes. **Mass should be on the vertical axis and length or area on the** horizontal axis. The origin should be (0,0).

2 Physics Lab

2. Analyzing Graphs Identify the relationship between the variables. Do your graphs depict linear, quadratic, or inverse relationships? How do you know? Can you calculate the slope of each graph? Organize, analyze, evaluate, and make inferences in trends from your data. Predict from the trends in your data whether or not your graphs will go through the origin (0,0). Should they?
The graph depicts a linear relationship. Slope = mass/length and slope = mass/area. The graph should pass through the origin. When the length or area is zero, the mass is zero.

3. Calculating Results Write the equations that relate your variables. Use the equations and the graphs to predict the unknown mass of wire and floor tile.

mass = *k*(area)

mass = *k'*(length)

The unknown masses will depend upon the samples available.

4. Checking Your Hypothesis Measure the unknown masses of the wire and floor tile on the balance. Do your measurements agree with the predicted values?
Most students will find the measured masses to be within the uncertainty of the predictions made from their graphs and equations.

5. Calculating Results Use a computer plotting program or a graphing calculator to re-plot your data and find the equations that relate your variables. Are the equations the same as you found earlier?
Students should find that the equations are the same as before.

Apply

1. Suppose another group measures longer wires. How should the slope of your graph compare to their slope?
Their graph would be more spread out than yours, but your data should fit on their line because both graphs should have the same slope and both should go through the origin.

2. In the pharmaceutical industry, how might the weight of compressed medicine tablets be used to determine the quantity of finished tablets produced in a specific lot?
The average weight for a certain number of tablets, for example ten tablets, is found, then the total weight of the finished tablet lot is determined. The finished number of tablets is calculated by dividing the average weight per tablet into the total weight. This procedure is used because an average lot size can be 1 million or more tablets.

2-1 Pocket Lab

How good is your eye?

The distance from your nose to your outstretched fingertips is about 1 m. Estimate the distance between you and three objects in the room. Have the members in your lab group each make a data table and record their estimates. Verify each distance.

Compare Results

Were the estimates reasonably close? Did one person consistently make accurate estimates? What could be done to improve your accuracy?
Accuracy will vary but should improve with practice.

2-2

![Pocket Lab]

How far around?

Use a meterstick to measure the diameter of four circular objects and a string to measure their circumferences. Record your data in a table. Graph the circumference versus the diameter.

Communicate Results

Write a few sentences to summarize your graph. Write a sentence using the word that explains the meaning of the slope of your graph. Explain whether the value of the slope would be different if you had measured in different units.

The graph shows a linear relationship. The slope of the graph should be about 3.14. The linear

relationship can be expressed as *circumference* = 3.14 *(diameter)*. **Some students may recognize**

this as the formula for finding the circumference of a circle. The slope, *circumference/diameter,*

equals pi. The value of the slope of this graph does not depend on the units of measurement.

_____

_____

_____

_____

_____

_____

---

3 Design Your Own Physics Lab

Notion of Motion

Problem

You are to construct motion diagrams based on a steady walk and a simulated sprint.

Hypothesis

Devise a procedure for creating motion diagrams for a steady walk and a sprint.

Students may think that the sprinter should reach a mark at the end of

each second just as the walker does.

Plan the Experiment

1. Decide on the variables to be measured and how you will measure them.
2. Decide how you will measure the distance over the course of the walk.
3. Create a data table.

Data and Observations				
Steady Walk				
distance				
time				
velocity				

4. Organize team members to perform the individual tasks of walker, sprinter, timekeeper, and recorder.
5. **Check the Plan** Make sure your teacher approves your final plan before you proceed.
6. Think about how the procedures you use for the fast sprint may differ from those you used for the steady walk, then follow steps 1–5.
7. Dispose of, recycle, or put away materials as appropriate.

Analyze and Conclude

1. **Organizing Data** Use your data to write a word description of each event.

The walker had a steady velocity, but the velocity of the sprinter

was increasing.

Possible Materials

stopwatch
metersticks
10-m length of string,
cord, or tape

3-1 Pocket Lab

Rolling Along

Tape a 2.5- to 3-m strip of paper to the floor or other smooth, level surface. Gently roll a smooth rubber or steel ball along the paper so that it takes about 4 or 5 s to cover the distance. Now roll the ball while a recorder makes beeps every 1.0 s. Mark the paper at the position of the rolling ball every 1.0 s.

Analyze and Conclude

Are the marks on the paper evenly spaced? Make a data table of position and time and use the data to plot a graph. In a few sentences, describe the graph.

The slope of the graph decreases with time, which indicates that the velocity of the ball is

decreasing.

_____

_____

_____

_____

_____

---

3 Physics Lab

2. **Comparing Results** Describe the data in the velocity portion of the WALK portion of the experiment. Then describe the data in the velocity portion of the SPRINT portion of the experiment. **Each entry for velocity in the WALK portion was about the same for each time interval. The**

entries in the SPRINT portion increased as time passed.

3. **Comparing Data** Make a motion diagram for each event. Label the diagrams *Begin* and *End* to indicate the beginning and the end of the motion.

4. **Organizing Data** Draw the acceleration vectors on your motion diagram for the two events.

5. **Comparing Results** Compare the pattern of average velocity vectors for the two events. How are they different? Explain. **The velocity vectors are all the same length for the walk, but for the sprint, they start short**

and become longer with each second.

6. **Inferring Conclusions** Compare the acceleration vectors from the steady walk and the sprint. What can you conclude? **The sprinter is accelerating, but the acceleration of the walker is zero.**

Apply

1. Imagine that you have a first-row seat for the 100-m world championship sprint. Write a description of the race in terms of velocity and acceleration. Include a motion diagram that would represent the race run by the winner. **The sprinter runs with increasing velocity and acceleration.**

3-2 Pocket Lab

Swinging

Use a camcorder to capture an object swinging like a pendulum. Then attach a piece of tracing paper or other see-through material over the TV screen as you play back the video frame by frame. Use a felt marker to show the position of the center of the swinging object at every frame as it moves from one side of the screen to the opposite side.

Analyze and Conclude

Does the object have a steady speed? Describe how the speed changes. Where is the object moving the fastest? Do you think that your results are true for other swinging objects? Why? **The object has its greatest speed at the center; its smallest speed at the extreme positions of its travel. It does not have a steady speed.**

---

4 Physics Lab

The Paper River

Problem

How does a boat travel on a river?

Procedure

1. Your car will serve as the boat. Write a brief statement to explain how the boat's speed can be determined. **In order to calculate speed, displacement and time must be measured.**

2. Your boat will start with all wheels on the paper river. Measure the width of the river and predict how much time is needed for your boat to go directly across the river. Show your data and calculations. **Student predictions will vary.**

3. Determine the time needed to cross the river when your boat is placed on the edge of the river. Make three trials and record the times.

4. Using the average of your trials, construct a graph showing the position and time for the boat crossing the river. If possible, use a computer or calculator to create the graph. Use this graph to observe and identify the relationship between variables.

5. Do you think it will take the boat more or less time to cross when the river is flowing? Explain your prediction. **Student predictions will vary.**

6. Have a student (the hydro engineer) walk slowly, at a constant speed, while pulling the river along the floor. Each group should measure the time it takes for the boat to cross the flowing river. Make three trials and record the times. Compare the results with your prediction. **Data will vary.**

7. Using the grid from Step 4 and the average of your data from Step 6, construct a graph showing the position and time for the boat crossing the river when the river is flowing. Use a different color for the plot than you did for the boat without the river flowing.

Materials

🔋 small battery-powered car (or physics bulldozer)

meterstick

protractor

stopwatch

a piece of paper, 1 m × 10 m

4 Physics Lab

8. Devise a method to measure the speed of the river. Have the hydro engineer pull the river at a constant speed and collect the necessary data.
Answers will vary.

9. Save the paper for later classes to use or recycle it.

Data and Observations

Table 1

Moving River			
Trial #	Time (s)	Trial #	Time (s)

1. Does the boat move in the direction that it is pointing?
The motion of the boat is a combination of its own speed and the speed of the river.

2. Analyze and evaluate the trends in your data. How did the graphs of position versus time compare?
The graphs should be nearly the same.

3. Infer from the trends in your data if the motion of the water affected the time needed to cross when the boat was pointed straight to the far shore. **No, the same time is needed. The river does not push or pull the boat in the direction called "across the river." Therefore, the motion of the river cannot affect the "across" motion of the boat.**

4. Based on the trends in your data, predict whether the river or the boat had the greater speed. Explain your choice.
Student data will vary depending on the speed of the river and the vehicle.

Analyze and Conclude

1. **Calculating Results** Calculate the speed of the river.
Data will vary.

---

4 Physics Lab

2. **Inferring Conclusions** Using your results for the speed of the boat and the speed of the river, calculate the speed of the boat compared to the ground when the boat is headed directly downstream and directly upstream.
Answers will vary.

The combined downstream speed is the vector sum:

ground speed = boat speed + river speed.

The combined upstream speed is the vector difference:

ground speed = boat speed − river speed.

Note: The boat cannot go upstream when the current is faster than the boat.

The combined speed is the vector sum: ground speed = boat speed − river speed.

Apply

1. Do small propeller aircraft always move in the direction that they are pointing? Do they ever fly sideways?
The motion of a plane is the combination of its speed through the air and the speed of the air (wind). Whenever a plane is flying at an angle to the wind, it will not be moving in the direction that it is pointing.

2. Try the lab again using a battery-powered boat on a small stream.
Students should get similar results.

Physics: Principles and Problems

Teacher Guide and Answers **7T**

14 *Physics Lab and Pocket Lab Worksheets*

Physics: Principles and Problems

Physics: Principles and Problems

Physics Lab and Pocket Lab Worksheets 15

4-1 Pocket Lab

Ladybug

You notice a ladybug moving from one corner of your textbook to the corner diagonally opposite. The trip takes the ladybug 6.0 s. Use the long side of the book as the x-axis. Find the component vectors of the ladybug's velocity, v_x and v_y, and the resultant velocity R.

Analyze and Conclude

Does the ladybug's path from one corner to the other affect the values in your measurements or calculations? Do $v_x + v_y$ really add up to R? Explain. **The path of the ladybug does not affect the calculations. The vector sum of v_x and v_y is the resultant R, which is the velocity of the ladybug.**

_____

_____

_____

_____

---

5 Design Your Own Physics Lab

Ball and Car Race

Problem

A car moving along a highway passes a parked police car with a radar detector. Just as the car passes, the police car starts to pursue, moving with a constant acceleration. The police car catches up with the car just as it leaves the jurisdiction of the police officer.

Hypothesis

Sketch the position-versus-time graphs and the velocity-versus-time graphs for this chase, then simulate the chase.

Plan the Experiment

1. Identify the variables in this activity.

2. Determine how you will give the ball a constant acceleration.

3. Devise a method to ensure that both objects reach the end of the track at the same time.

4. Construct a data table that will show the positions of both objects at the beginning, the halfway point, and the end of the chase.

5. **Check the Plan** Review your plan with your teacher before you begin the race.

6. Construct p-t and v-t graphs for both objects. Use technology to construct these graphs if possible. Identify the relationships between variables.

7. Dispose of materials that cannot be reused or recycled. Put away materials that can be used again.

Possible Materials

battery-powered car
1-in. steel ball
masking tape
stopwatch
wood block
graph paper
90-cm-long grooved track

5-1

Pocket Lab

Uniform or Not?

Set up a U-channel on a book so that it acts as an inclined ramp, or make a channel from two meter-sticks taped together along the edges. Release a steel ball so that it rolls down the ramp. Using a stop-watch, measure the time it takes the ball to roll 0.40 m.

Analyze and Conclude

Write a brief description of the motion of the ball. Predict how much time it would take the ball to roll 0.80 m. Explain your prediction. **Many students will predict that the time needed to roll twice as far will be twice as much. Some will suggest that the time will be more than twice. The actual time is less than twice.**

---

5   Physics Lab

Analyze and Conclude

1. **Comparing and Contrasting** Compare the velocities of the cars at the beginning and at the end of the chase. Write a verbal description. **The car has a steady velocity. At the beginning of the chase, the police car has zero velocity. At the end of the chase, the police car is moving twice as fast as the speeder.**

2. **Using Graphs** At any time during the chase, did the cars ever have the same velocity? If so, mark these points on the graphs. **Both cars had the same velocity at the halfway time, not the halfway position.**

3. **Comparing and Contrasting** Compare the average velocity of the police car to that of the car. **Both cars had the same change in position in the same time interval and, therefore, had the same average velocities.**

4. **Calculating Results** Calculate the average speed of each car. **A typical speed for the car is between 20 cm/s and 35 cm/s.**

Apply

1. Explain why it took the police car so long to catch the car after it sped by. **It took several seconds for the police car to reach the speed of the car. During that time, the distance between the cars was increasing.**

2. Analyze and evaluate the plots of the speeder's motion. Infer from the plots the speeder's acceleration. **Data will vary. The acceleration is found by calculating the slope of the v-t graph.**

3. If the speeder accelerated at the exact same rate of the police car at the moment the speeder passes the police car, would the police car ever catch the speeder? Predict how your graphs would change. **No. The graphs would be parallel lines.**

4. Develop a CBL lab that plots velocity of a non-accelerated object and an accelerated object. Describe your graphs. **Labs will vary. The v-t graph of a non-accelerated object is a horizontal line, while for an accelerated object, the graph is a slanted line.**

5-2

Pocket Lab

A Ball Race

Assemble an inclined ramp from a piece of U-channel or two metersticks taped together. Make a mark at 40 cm from the top and another at 80 cm from the top. If two balls are released at the same instant, one ball from the top and the other ball at 40 cm, will the balls get closer or farther apart as they roll down the ramp? Why? Try it. Now, release one ball from the top and then release another ball from the top as soon as the first ball reaches the 40-cm mark.

Analyze and Conclude

Explain your observations in terms of velocities. Do the balls ever have the same velocities as they roll down the hill? Do they have the same acceleration?

Some students will predict that the top ball will gain on the bottom ball. These students are

confusing velocity with acceleration. The velocity of the balls increases as they roll, but the

acceleration is the same for both balls because it depends upon the steepness of the ramp.

_____

_____

_____

_____

5-3

Pocket Lab

Bowling Ball Displacement

Take a bowling ball and three stopwatches into the hallway. Divide into three groups. Have all timers start their watches when the ball is rolled. Group 1 should stop its watch when the ball has gone 10 m, group 2 should stop its watch when the ball has rolled 20 m, and group 3 should stop its watch when the ball has rolled 30 m.

Analyze and Conclude

Record the data and calculate the average speed for each distance. Could the average speed for 30 m be used to predict the time needed to roll 100 m? Why or why not?

Students will not be able to predict the time needed to roll 100 m from the average speed for 30 m

because the ball is slowing down, not traveling with constant velocity.

_____

_____

_____

_____

5-4 Pocket Lab

Direction of Acceleration

Tape a bubble level onto the top of a laboratory cart. Center the bubble. Observe the direction of the motion of the bubble as you pull the cart forward, move it at constant speed, and allow it to coast to a stop. Relate the motion of the bubble to the acceleration of the cart. Predict what would happen if you tie the string to the back of the cart and repeat the experiment. Try it.

Analyze and Conclude

Draw motion diagrams for the cart as you moved it in the forward direction and it coasted to a stop and as you repeated the experiment in the opposite direction.

Students' motion diagrams should reflect the fact that objects moving in a straight line at a steady speed have zero acceleration; that when an object is speeding up, the acceleration is in the direction of the object's motion; and that when an object is slowing down, the acceleration is opposite the direction of the object's motion.

---

6 Physics Lab

The Elevator Ride

Problem

Why do you feel heavier or lighter when riding in an elevator?

Procedure

1. Imagine that you take an upward elevator ride. Write a few sentences describing when you feel normal, heavier than normal, and lighter than normal. Repeat for a downward elevator ride.

2. Hold the 1-kg mass in your hand and give it an upward elevator ride. Describe when the mass feels normal, heavier than normal, and lighter than normal.

3. Hold the mass in your hand and give it a downward elevator ride. Describe when the mass feels normal, heavier than normal, and lighter than normal.

4. Securely tape the mass to the hook on the spring scale. **CAUTION:** *A falling mass can cause serious damage to feet or toes.*

5. Start with the mass just above the floor and take it on an upward and then a downward elevator ride.

6. When complete, unwrap the tape and throw it away. Put away the mass and the spring scale.

Materials

1-kg mass

20-N spring scale

10 cm masking tape

6 Physics Lab

3. **Interpreting Data** Identify those places in the ride when the spring scale records a lighter value. Which direction is the F_{net}? Which direction is the acceleration? **When starting downward (or moving upward but slowing), the floor must push with less force than the normal weight. F_{net} is downward and the acceleration is downward. The rider feels lighter.**

Apply

1. Based on the trends in your data, predict how riding in an elevator while standing on a scale will affect your weight measurement. Try it, and describe the forces on you. **While accelerating downward in an elevator, the scale will read less because the net force is downward. While accelerating upward, the scale will read more because the net force is upward. When moving at a constant speed, the rider will feel normal.**

2. Do you feel heavier or lighter when riding on an escalator? Explain your answer in terms of the motion and the forces. **Except during the momentary acceleration when stepping on or off the escalator, you should feel your normal weight. The escalator moves at a steady speed. The forces are balanced.**

3. Identify the places on a roller coaster where you feel heavier or lighter. Explain your answer in terms of the motion and the forces. **The riders feel lighter when they are accelerating downward. This occurs when the coaster is "falling" down a hill. The riders feel heavier when they are accelerating upward. This occurs as the coaster begins climbing a hill.**

---

6 Physics Lab

Data and Observations

Table 1			
Place in the Ride	Scale Reading (N)	Place in the Ride	Scale Reading (N)

1. Watch the spring scale and record the readings for different parts of the ride.

Analyze and Conclude

1. **Interpreting Data** Identify those places in the ride when the spring scale records a normal value for the mass. Describe the motion of the mass. Are the forces balanced or unbalanced? **When moving at a steady speed, the forces are balanced, meaning that F_{net} = 0. The rider will feel her normal weight.**

2. **Interpreting Data** Identify those places in the ride when the spring scale records a heavier value. Which direction is the F_{net}? Which direction is the acceleration? **When starting upward (or moving downward but slowing), the floor must push with more force than the normal weight. F_{net} is upward and the acceleration is upward. The rider feels heavier.**

6-1

Pocket Lab

How far is forever?

Galileo proposed that if a perfectly smooth ball were rolled on a perfectly smooth surface in a vacuum, it would roll forever at a steady speed. Use a stopwatch with a lap or split timer and measure the time it takes a ball to roll the first meter and then the total time it takes to roll 2.0 m.

Analyze and Conclude

Make a motion diagram to describe the motion and a free-body diagram showing the forces acting on the ball. Indicate the direction of the net force, F_{net}, and the acceleration.

The motion diagram shows a shorter arrow for the second part of the roll. The forces acting on the ball are the downward force of gravity, the upward force of the table, and the force of friction, which is in the direction opposite the motion of the ball. Because the ball is slowing down, the acceleration and the net force are also in the direction opposite the motion of the ball.

6-2

Pocket Lab

Tug-of-War Challenge

In a tug-of-war, predict how the force you exert on your end of the rope compares to the force your opponent exerts if you pull and your opponent just holds the end of the rope. Predict how the forces compare if the rope moves in your direction. Try it.

Analyze and Conclude

What did you notice about the forces? What happened when you started to move your opponent in your direction?

Holding is the same as pulling. Even when your opponent starts moving, the forces on the rope are still at the same reading.

_____

_____

_____

_____

_____

6-3

Pocket Lab

Friction depends on what?

Find out! Tape a 0.5-kg mass to a 10-cm × 10-cm piece of cardboard. Tie one end of a string to the mass and the other end to a spring scale. Pull until the mass begins to move. Record the maximum force before the mass began to slide as the static force of friction. Repeat for a 1.0-kg mass. Repeat with the two masses on a 10-cm × 20-cm piece of cardboard.

Analyze and Conclude

Describe your results. Does the force of friction depend on the mass? Does the force of friction depend on the surface area?

The static friction force is proportional to the mass. The surface area has little effect on the amount

of static friction.

_____
_____
_____
_____
_____
_____
_____
_____
_____
_____

6-4

Pocket Lab

Upside-Down Parachute

How long does it take for a falling object to reach a terminal velocity? How fast is the terminal velocity? Does the terminal velocity depend on the mass? Find out. Use coffee filters, a meterstick, a stopwatch, and your creativity to answer each question.

Analyze and Conclude

Describe your procedures, results, and conclusions to the class.

Student data will vary, but students should conclude that the terminal velocity does not depend

upon mass.

_____
_____
_____
_____
_____
_____
_____
_____
_____
_____
_____
_____
_____

6-5

Pocket Lab

Stopping Forces

Tie two 1-m long strings to the backs of two lab carts and attach 0.2 kg masses to the other ends. Hang the masses over the end of a lab table so that the masses are just above the floor. Add mass to one of the carts so that its mass is about twice its original mass. Predict how the motion of the carts might be different when you push them at the same speed and then let them coast. Try it. Predict how you could change the mass on one of the strings so that the motion of the carts would be the same when given the same initial speed. Test your prediction.

Analyze and Conclude

Describe your observations in words and in a motion diagram. Explain your results in terms of inertia, force, mass, and acceleration.

A motion diagram shows shorter velocity vectors in each time interval for the heavier cart compared to the lighter cart. The acceleration vector is also shorter for the heavier cart. With

increased mass on the string of the heavier cart, the two carts have equal acceleration.

_____

_____

_____

_____

Design Your Own
1 Physics Lab

The Softball Throw

Problem

What advice can you give the center fielder on your softball team on how to throw the ball to the catcher at home plate so that it gets there before the runner?

Hypothesis

Formulate a hypothesis using what you know about the horizontal and vertical motion of a projectile to advise the center fielder about how to throw the ball. Consider the factors that affect the time it will take for the ball to arrive at home plate.

Student hypotheses may reflect that the ball must be thrown at an

angle of 45°.

_____

_____

Possible Materials

stopwatch

softball

football field or large open area with premeasured distances

Plan the Experiment

1. As a group, determine the variable(s) you want to measure. How do horizontal and vertical velocity affect the range?

2. Who will time the throws? How will you determine the range? Will the range be a constant or a variable? How many trials will you complete?

3. Construct a data table or spreadsheet for recording data from all the trial throws. Record all your calculations in a table.

Data and Observations

Table 1

	Time (t) (seconds)	Horizontal Velocity (v_x)(m/s)	Vertical Velocity (v_y) (m/s)	Initial Velocity (v_0) (m/s)
Range (R) (meters)				
Trial 1				
Trial 2				

4. **Check the Plan** Make sure your teacher approves your final plan before you proceed.

7-1

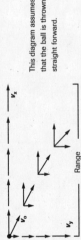

Pocket Lab

Over the Edge

Obtain two balls, one twice the mass of the other. Predict which ball will hit the floor first when you roll them over the surface of a table with the same speed and let them roll off. Predict which ball will hit the floor farther from the table. Explain your predictions.

_____
_____
_____
_____
_____

Analyze and Conclude

Does the mass of the ball affect its motion? Is mass a factor in any of the equations for projectile motion?
No, mass is not a factor in any of the equations for projectile motion.

_____
_____
_____

7

_____ Name _____

Physics Lab

Analyze and Conclude

1. **Analyzing Data** How can your data be used to determine values for v_x and v_y?

   $R = v_x t; v_x = R/t$

   $0 = \frac{1}{2}gt^2 + v_y t; v_y = -\frac{1}{2}gt$

2. **Diagramming the Results** Draw a diagram that shows the relationship between R, v_x, v_y, and v_0.

   This diagram assumes that the ball is thrown straight forward.

3. **Calculating Results** Determine the initial values for v_x and v_y. Use the Pythagorean theorem to find the value of the initial velocity, v_0, for each trial.

   Typical data: $R = 60$ m, $t = 4.0$ s

   $v_x = 60$ m/4.0 s $= 15$ m/s

   $v_y = 9.80$ m/s$^2 \times 2.0$ s $= 20$ m/s

   $v = 25$ m/s

4. **Analyzing Data** Was the range of each person's throw about the same? Did the initial velocity of the throws vary?
   Range and initial velocity vary.

5. **Analyzing Data** Analyze and evaluate the trends in your data. How did the angle at which the ball was thrown affect the range? The time?
   Neglecting friction, the largest range will be reached for angles near 45°. In practice, the angle will be less than 45° because of the starting height above the ground, friction, and the physiology of the shoulder.

6. **Checking Your Hypothesis** Should the center fielder throw the ball to the catcher at home plate with a larger v_x or v_y?
   Throws at angles less than 45° will have $v_x > v_y$. If v_x is great enough, the ball will reach home plate in a shorter amount of time.

Apply

1. Infer from the trends in your data why a kickoff in a football game might be made at a different angle than a punt.
   The most important factor in the kickoff is distance. On punts, the time in the air is often as important as the distance. Punts are purposely kicked at a large angle.

Date ———— Period ———— Name ————

1-2

Pocket Lab

Where the Ball Bounces

Place a golf ball in your hand and extend your arm sideways so that the ball is at shoulder height. Drop the ball and have a lab partner start a stopwatch when the ball strikes the floor and stop it the next time the ball strikes the floor. Predict where the ball will hit when you walk at a steady speed and drop the ball. Would the ball take the same time to bounce? Try it.

Analyze and Conclude

Where does the ball hit? Does it take more time?

The ball hits the floor alongside the student. The ball takes the same amount of time to bounce as before because its vertical velocity and acceleration are not affected by its horizontal motion.

Date ———— Period ———— Name ————

1-3

Pocket Lab

Target Practice

Tie a 1.0-m length of string onto a one-hole rubber stopper. **Note:** Everyone in the classroom should be wearing goggles. Swing the stopper around your head in a horizontal circle. Release the string from your hand when the string is lined up with a spot on the wall. Repeat the experiment until the stopper flies toward the spot on the wall.

Analyze and Conclude

Did the stopper travel toward the spot on the wall? What does this indicate about the direction of the velocity compared to the orientation of the string?

When the stopper was released as it aligned radially outward with the spot on the wall, it did not hit the spot. The stopper's velocity is always perpendicular to the orientation of the string.

8 Physics Lab

The Orbit

Problem

How does the gravitational force vary at different points of an elliptical orbit?

Procedure

1. Place the paper on top of the cardboard. Push the pushpins into the paper and cardboard so that they are between 7 and 10 cm apart. Push the pushpins into the paper and cardboard so that they are between 7 and 10 cm apart.
2. Make a loop with the string. Place the loop over the two pushpins. Keep the loop tight as you draw the ellipse, as shown on page 179 in your textbook.
3. Remove the pins and string. Draw a small star centered at one of the pinholes.
4. Draw the position of a planet in the orbit where it is farthest from the star. Measure and record the distance from this position to the center of the star.
5. Draw a 1-cm-long force vector from this planet directly toward the star. Label this vector 1.0 F.
6. Draw the position of a planet when it is nearest the star. Measure and record the distance from this position to the star's center.

Materials

🖐

2 pushpins

21-cm × 28-cm piece of cardboard or corkboard

sheet of paper

30-cm piece of string or thread

pencil

metric ruler

Data and Observations

Table 1	
Farthest Distance	
Nearest Distance	

Analyze and Conclude

1. **Calculating Results** Calculate the amount of force on the planet at the closest distance. Gravity is an inverse square force. If the planet is 0.45 times as far as the closest distance, the force is $1/(0.45)^2$ as much, or 4.9 F. Hint: The force will be more than 1.0 F.

   Students' calculations and vector diagrams will vary depending on their drawings.

7-4 Pocket Lab

Falling Sideways

🖐

Will a ball dropped straight down hit the floor before or after a ball that is tossed directly sideways at the same instant? Try it. You may need to repeat the experiment several times before you are sure of your results. Toss the ball sideways and not up or down.

Analyze and Conclude

Compare the downward force on each ball. Compare the distance that each ball falls in the vertical direction.

If the balls have the same mass, they experience the same downward gravitational force. Both balls experience the same acceleration due to gravity and fall the same distance, so they hit the floor simultaneously.

_____

_____

_____

_____

_____

_____

8 Physics Lab

2. Diagramming Results Draw the force vector, using the correct length and direction, for this position and at two other positions in the orbit. Use the scale 1.0 F : 1.0 cm.

Apply

1. Draw a velocity vector at each planet position to show the direction of motion. Assume that the planet moves in a clockwise pattern on the ellipse. Predict where the planet moves fastest. Use an orbital motion simulation program for a computer to verify your prediction. **The planet moves fastest when closest to the star. The velocity vectors should be tangent to the ellipse.**

2. Look at the direction of the velocity vectors and the direction of the force vectors at each position of the planet. Infer where the planet gains and loses speed. Explain your reasoning. **The planet gains speed as it approaches the star and loses speed as it moves away from the star. At the nearest and farthest positions, the force is perpendicular to velocity. At these points, the force changes direction but not the speed of the planet.**

8-1 Pocket Lab

Strange Orbit

Does the moon affect the motion of Earth in its orbit around the sun? Make your prediction. Then, build the following model planet and moon system. Push a small ball of clay onto the end of a drinking straw to represent the moon. Push a larger ball of clay, representing the planet, onto the opposite end. Tape a piece of string to the balance point on the straw so that the straw will stay parallel to the table when it is lifted. Give the moon a gentle push so that it moves in a slow circle.

Analyze and Conclude

Does the planet move in response to the motion of the moon? What effect would a more massive moon have on the planet? What might you conclude about Earth's motion? **Increasing the mass of the moon would cause the balance point to move farther from the planet and therefore produce a more noticeable wobble in the orbit.**

8-2 *Pocket Lab*

Weight in a Free Fall

Tie a string to the top of a spring scale. Hang a 1.0-kg mass on the spring scale. Hold the scale in your hand.

Analyze and Conclude

Observe the weight of the mass. What will the reading be when the string is released (as the mass and scale are falling)? Why?

The reading on the falling spring scale will be zero. Students should indicate that that the force went to zero quickly. The mass is accelerating downward. The mass is in apparent weightlessness.

_____

_____

_____

_____

_____

_____

8-3 *Pocket Lab*

Water, Water, Everywhere

This activity is best done outdoors. Use a pencil to poke a hole in the bottom and side of a cup. Hold your fingers over the two holes as you pour colored water into the cup until it is two-thirds full. Predict what will happen as the cup is allowed to fall. Drop the cup and watch closely.

Analyze and Conclude

What happened? Why?

When the cup is dropped, the water stays in the cup. There is no pressure between the falling cup and the water inside it. Both the cup and the water are being accelerated the same by gravity. The water and cup are in apparent weightlessness.

_____

_____

_____

_____

_____

_____

9 ⟊ Physics Lab

The Explosion

Problem

How do the forces and changes in momenta acting on different masses compare during an explosion?

Materials

two laboratory carts (one with a spring mechanism)
two C-clamps
two blocks of wood
20-N spring balance
0.50-kg mass
stopwatch
masking tape
meterstick

Procedure

1. Securely tape the 0.50-kg mass to cart 2 and then use the balance to determine the mass of each cart.

2. Use the C-clamps to secure the two blocks of wood to the laboratory table. Position the blocks at least 1 m apart.

3. Arrange the equipment as shown in the diagram.

4. Predict the starting position so that the carts will hit the blocks at the same instant when the spring mechanism is released.

5. Place pieces of tape on the table at the front of the carts to mark starting positions.

6. Depress the mechanism to release the spring and explode the carts.

7. Notice which cart hits the block first.

8. Adjust the starting position for the carts until they hit the wood blocks at the same time. Be sure to mark the starting position of each cart for each trial. Measure the time it takes the carts to reach the blocks.

9. Dispose of the masking tape and put the other materials away.

Data and Observations

1. Which cart moved farther? How do you know?
   The less massive cart traveled farther. The distance from the

   starting point to the wood block was greater.

2. Which cart moved faster? Explain.
   The less massive cart moved faster. It traveled a greater distance

   in the same amount of time as the more massive cart.

Analyze and Conclude

1. **Analyzing** Which data will help you estimate the velocity of each cart? Explain.
   The distance traveled and the travel time can be used to estimate

   the velocity of each cart.

---

9 Physics Lab

2. **Estimating** Which cart had the greater velocity?
   Assuming a typical laboratory cart has a mass of about 1.0 kg, the 1.0-kg cart will travel

   about 1.5 times the speed of the 1.5-kg cart.

3. **Comparing** Compare the change in momentum of each cart.
   Each cart will have equal (but opposite) changes in momentum.

4. **Applying** Suppose that the spring pushed on cart 1 for 0.05 s. How long did cart 2 push on the spring? Explain.
   The times of interaction must be equal.

5. **Comparing** Using $F\Delta t = m\Delta v$, which cart had the greater impulse?
   The average force on the carts depends on the individual spring. Typical values may be in the

   range of 10 to 25 N. The forces on the carts must be equal (but opposite).

Apply

1. Based on your data, explain why a target shooter might prefer to shoot a more massive gun.
   Target shooters know that a more massive gun will recoil less than a less massive gun. For a

   given change of momentum, the change of velocity will be less for a gun with greater mass.

9-1

Pocket Lab

Cart Momentum

Attach a spring scale to a laboratory cart. First, pull the cart for 1.0 s while exerting 1.0 N of force. Next, pull the cart for 2.0 s while exerting about 0.50 N of force. Predict which trial will give the cart more acceleration. Explain.

Trial 1 will produce more acceleration because the force is larger ($a = F/m$).

Predict which trial will give the cart more velocity. Explain.

Both trials will produce the same change in velocity.

Then try it.

Recognizing Cause and Effect

Which factor, F or Δt, seems to be more important in changing the velocity of the cart?

Students will find that both trials resulted in the same velocity. The F and the Δt are equally important.

9-2

Pocket Lab

Skateboard Fun

Have two students sit facing each other on skateboards approximately 3 to 5 m apart. Place a rope in their hands. Predict what will happen when one student pulls on the rope while the other just holds his or her end. Explain your prediction. Which person is exerting more force on the rope?

Students should realize that one cannot pull without the other pulling.

Compare the amount of time that the force is acting on each person. Which person will have a greater change in momentum? Explain.

Then try it. Describe what really happened.

Design an Experiment

Can you devise a method to pull only one student to the other so that the other student doesn't move?

Students may attach the ends of the rope to a large spring balance and repeat the activity. Both students will accelerate toward each other. Equal (but opposite) forces act for equal times. The students will have equal (but opposite) changes in momentum. There should be no way to pull one student to the other, unless one student is fixed to the floor.

10 Design Your Own
Physics Lab

Your Power

Problem

Can you estimate the power that you generate as you climb stairs? Climbing stairs requires energy. As you move your weight through a distance, you accomplish work. The rate at which you do this work is power.

Hypothesis

Form a hypothesis that relates estimating power to measurable quantities. Predict the difficulties you may encounter as you are trying to solve the problem.

I can estimate power by measuring my weight, the height of the stairs, and the time it takes to climb the stairs. Difficulties include neglecting your forward push against the internal resistance of your body, accurately measuring the height of the stairs, and estimating mass.

Plan the Experiment

In your group, develop a plan to measure your power as you climb stairs. Be prepared to present your plan, your data, your calculations, and your results to the rest of the class. Take measurements for at least two students.

1. Identify the dependent and independent variables.
2. Describe your procedures.
3. Set up data tables.
4. Write any equations that you will need for the calculations.
5. **Check the Plan** Show your teacher your plan before you leave the room to start the experiment.

Analyze and Conclude

1. **Calculating Results** Show your calculations for the power rating of each climber.
   Typical power ratings should be in the range of 100 to 300 W.

Possible Materials

Determine which variables you will measure and then plan a procedure for taking measurements. Tell your teacher what materials you would like to use to accomplish your plan. Once you have completed your lab, be sure to dispose of, recycle, or put away your materials.

---

10 Physics Lab

2. **Comparing Results** Did each climber have the same power rating?
   The power rating will be different for each climber.

3. **Analyzing Data** Explain how your power could be increased.
   A climber can improve his or her rating by climbing faster.

4. **Making Inferences** Explain why the fastest climber might not have the highest power rating. Explain why the largest climber might not have the highest power rating.
   The power rating depends on both the mass and the time.

Apply

1. Your local electric company charges you about 11 cents for a kilowatt-hour of energy. At this rate, how much money could you earn by climbing stairs continuously for one hour? Show your calculations.
   A typical student power rating is 250 W or 0.25 kW. This power from your electric company will cost only about 2.5 cents for one hour.

10-1

Pocket Lab

Working Out

Attach a spring scale to a 1.0-kg mass with a string. Pull the mass along the table at a slow, steady speed while keeping the scale parallel to the tabletop. Note the reading on the spring scale.

Analyze and Conclude

What are the physical factors that determine the amount of force? How much work is done in moving the mass 1.0 m? Predict the force and the work when a 2.0-kg mass is pulled along the table. Try it. Was your prediction accurate?

The reading on the scale is a measure of the sliding friction between the table and the mass. The smoothness of the table and the hardness of each surface affect the frictional force. The work done is the average force times the displacement.

_____
_____
_____
_____
_____

10-2

Pocket Lab

An Inclined Mass

Attach a spring scale to a 1.0-kg mass with a string. Increase the angle between the string and the table-top, for example, to 30°. Try to keep the angle constant as you pull the 1.0-kg mass along the table at a slow, steady speed. Note the reading on the scale.

Analyze and Conclude

How much force is in the direction of motion? How much work is done when the 1.0-kg mass moves 1.0 m? How does the work compare to the previous value?

The reading on the scale is greater than when the 1.0-kg mass was pulled with a horizontal force.

The force in the direction of motion is almost the same as before. The work equals the horizontal component of the force times 1.0 m. The work is close to twice the previous value.

_____
_____
_____
_____
_____
_____

10-3

Pocket Lab

Wheel and Axle

The gear mechanism on your bicycle multiplies the distance that you travel. What does it do to the force? Try this activity to find out. Mount a wheel and axle on a solid support rod. Wrap a string clockwise around the small diameter wheel and a different string counterclockwise around the large diameter wheel. Hang a 500-g mass from the end of the string on the larger wheel. Pull the string down so that the mass is lifted by about 10 cm.

Analyze and Conclude

What did you notice about the force on the string in your hand? What did you notice about the distance that your hand needed to move to lift the mass? Explain the results in terms of the work done on both strings.

The force to hold the wheel will be equal to the weight of the mass (5.0 N) times the ratio of the wheel diameters. Pulling the string down a small distance will lift the mass a larger distance.

Again, the distances are in the ratio of the wheel diameters.

Design Your Own
Physics Lab

11

Down the Ramp

Problem

What factors affect the speed of a cart at the bottom of a ramp? Along the floor?

Hypothesis

Form a hypothesis that relates the speed or energy of the cart at the bottom of the ramp to the mass of the cart on the ramp.

Students should correctly hypothesize that when the cart starts higher on the hill, it will gain more speed on the ramp. The equation for gravitational potential energy is $U_g = mgh$. This value can be defined to be zero when the cart is on the floor. Some students will realize that the loss of potential energy should result in the gain in kinetic energy.

Plan the Experiment

1. Your lab group should develop a plan to answer the questions stated in the problem. How should you structure your investigation? How many trials do you need for each setup? Be prepared to present and defend your plan, data, and results to the class.

2. Identify the independent and dependent variables. Which will you keep constant?

3. Describe your procedures.

4. Describe the energy changes as the cart rolls down the ramp and onto the floor.

5. Construct data tables or spreadsheets that will show the measurements that you make.

6. **Check the Plan** Make sure your teacher has approved your plan before you proceed with your experiment.

7. When you have completed the lab, dispose of, recycle, or put away your materials.

Possible Materials

cart
0.50-kg mass
1.0-kg mass
board to be used as a ramp
stopwatch
meterstick
masking tape

11-1 Pocket Lab

Energy in Coins

Does your car require more or less stopping distance when it is loaded with passengers than when you are driving alone? A short activity will help you to answer this question. Lay a ruler on a smooth table. Place two quarters against the edge of the ruler. Momentarily push the two quarters at the same speed across the table, and then stop the ruler. The two quarters should slide the same distance before stopping. Now tape another coin on top of one quarter to increase its mass. Again push the coins with the ruler.

Analyze and Conclude

Does the stopping distance depend upon the mass? Explain.
The heavier coin has more kinetic energy, but because the normal force between the coin and the table is larger, the frictional force is larger. Therefore, more work is done for the same distance traveled. The same is true in the case of the cars. The heavier car has more kinetic energy, but the frictional force between its tires and the road is also larger, so more work is done in the same distance. The coins will stop in about the same distance. The heavier coin has more energy, but the force on it (friction) is proportionally greater.

_____

_____

_____

_____

_____

_____

---

11 Physics Lab

Analyze and Conclude

1. **Checking Your Hypothesis** Did the speed at the bottom of the ramp depend on the mass of the cart? Does twice the mass have twice the speed? Does three times the mass go three times as fast? **Students will find no significant difference in the speed when the mass is doubled or even tripled. There is more force on a larger mass, but the larger mass also has more inertia.**

2. **Calculating Results** List and explain the equations that you used for your energy calculations. What do the equations suggest about the speed at the bottom when the mass is changed?

   The equations are $U_g = mgh$ and $K = 1/2mv^2$. If students assume conservation of energy, then the loss of U_g equals the gain of K. The mass term cancels this out; this indicates that mass is not important in predicting the results.

3. **Comparing and Contrasting** Compare the gravitational potential energy of the cart at the starting position to the kinetic energy of the cart along the floor. What is your conclusion? **The starting potential energy of the cart on the hill might be set equal to the kinetic energy of the cart on the floor if there were no frictional losses.**

   _____

4. **Thinking Critically** Suppose one lab group finds that the cart has 30% more kinetic energy along the floor than the starting gravitational potential energy. What would you tell the group? **The conservation-of-energy concept does not allow a closed system to gain total energy. It is much more likely that the K of the cart on the floor will be 30% less.**

   _____

Apply

1. A Soap Box Derby is a contest in which riders coast down a long hill. Does the mass of the cart have a significant effect on the results? Predict what other factors may be more important in winning the race. **The mass of the car has only a small effect. The wheels are a crucial factor in winning a Soap Box Derby. The aerodynamics also are important, especially at faster speeds.**

_____

_____

11-2

Pocket Lab

Energy Exchange

Wear goggles for this activity. Select several different-sized steel balls and determine their masses. Stand a spring-loaded laboratory cart on end with the spring mechanism pointing upward. Place a ball on top of the spring mechanism. Press down on the ball to compress the spring until the ball is touching the cart. Quickly release the ball so that the spring shoots it upward. Repeat several times and measure the average height. Predict how high the other sizes of steel balls should go. Try it. Record the values in a data table.

Analyze and Conclude

Classify the balls in order of height attained. What conclusions can you reach?
Students will predict that the small ball will go about twice as high and the large ball will go half as

high. Students will find that the small ball does not go quite twice as high and the large ball goes a

little more than half as high. Some of the energy goes into moving the spring and the metal rod

attached to the spring.

_____

_____

_____

_____

_____

_____

_____

12

Physics Lab

Heating Up

Problem

How does a constant supply of thermal energy affect the temperature of water?

Procedure

1. Turn your hot plate to a medium setting (or as recommended by your teacher). Allow a few minutes for the plate to heat up. Wear goggles.

2. Pour 150 mL of room-temperature water into the 250-mL beaker.

3. Make a data and observations table.

4. Record the initial temperature of the water. The thermometer must not touch the bottom or sides of the beaker.

5. Place the beaker on the hot plate and record the temperature every 1.0 min. Carefully stir the water before taking a temperature reading.

6. Record the time when the water starts to boil. Continue recording the temperature for an additional 4.0 min.

7. Carefully remove the beaker from the hot plate. Record the temperature of the remaining water.

8. When you have completed the lab, dispose of the water as instructed by your teacher. Allow equipment to cool before putting it away.

Materials

hot plate (or Bunsen burner)

250-mL ovenproof glass beaker

water

thermometer

stopwatch

goggles

apron

Data and Observations

Table 1

Time	Temperature	Time	Temperature	Time	Temperature	Time	Temperature

Analyze and Conclude

1. **Analyzing Data** Make a graph of temperature (vertical axis) versus time (horizontal axis). Use a computer or a calculator to construct the graph if possible. What is the relationship between variables?

Sample graph:

The slope is fairly constant for the first few minutes. It is a linear relationship until the water boils, where it changes to a different linear relationship.

12-1  Pocket Lab

Melting

Label two foam cups A and B. Measure 75 mL of room-temperature water into each of the two cups. Add an ice cube to cup A. Add ice water to cup B until the water levels are equal. Measure the temperature of each cup at 1-min intervals until the ice has melted.

Analyze and Conclude

Do the samples reach the same final temperature? Why?
Many students will not believe the results. Even though the ice cube and the ice water are both at approximately 0°C, the ice will cool the water better than the ice water. The ice cube takes energy to change from a solid to a liquid.

---

12 Physics Lab

Name _____

2. **Interpreting Graphs** What is the slope of the graph for the first 3.0 minutes? Be sure to include units.
The slope of the graph depends on the amount of water and the setting of the hot plate.

3. **Relating Concepts** What is the thermal energy given to the water in the first 3.0 minutes?
Hint: $Q = mC\Delta T$.

Sample calculation: $Q = mC\Delta T$

$= (0.15 \text{ kg})(4180 \text{ J/kg °C})(70°C - 25°C)$

$= 2.8 \times 10^4 \text{ J}$

4. **Making Predictions** Use a dotted line on the same graph to predict what the graph would look like if the same procedure was followed with only half as much water.
The graph should have twice the slope.

Apply

1. Would you expect that the hot plate transferred energy to the water at a steady rate?
The setting on the hot plate was constant. The rate of energy flow into the water was probably constant.

2. Where is the energy going when the water is boiling?
After the water reached 100°C, all of the energy went into changing the water from a liquid into a gas.

12-2

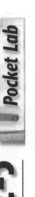

Pocket Lab

Cool Times

Place a 100-mL beaker in a 250-mL beaker. Put a thermometer in each beaker. Fill the small beaker with hot, colored water. Determine the temperature of the colored water. Slowly pour tap water into the large beaker until the water is at the same height in both beakers. Record the temperature in the large beaker. Record the temperature in both beakers every minute for 5 min. Plot your data for both beakers on a graph of temperature versus time. Measure and record the mass of water in each beaker.

Calculate and Conclude

Predict the final temperature. Describe each curve.

Students should predict that the final temperature will be between the hot and cold temperatures.

Because the specific heat of hot and cold water is the same, the equation used in calorimetry can

be simplified to $T_f = (m_A T_{Ai} + m_B T_{Bi})/(m_A + m_B)$. Students may find the measured temperature

lower than predicted by the equation because of energy lost by the hot water to the beakers and

the air. The curves should have a greater slope at the beginning when the temperatures are farthest

apart. Later, the changes in temperature will become smaller as the two temperatures gradually

approach each other.

12-3

Pocket Lab

Drip, Drip, Drip

Measure equal amounts of very hot and very cold water into two clear glasses (or beakers).

Hypothesize and Test

Predict what will happen if you simultaneously put one drop of food coloring in each glass. Try it. What happened? Why? Was the mixing symmetric?

Many students will predict that the rate of mixing will be different. Students will be surprised to see

how quickly the coloring mixes in the hot water. The mixing is faster in the hot water because the

molecules have a higher average speed. The mixing is not symmetric due to the random motion of

the molecules.

Physics: Principles and Problems

Teacher Guide and Answers **29T**

13 〰️ Physics Lab

Float or Sink?

Problem

How can you measure the buoyancy of objects?

Materials

beaker
water
film canister with lid
25 pennies
250-g spring scale
pan balance

Procedure

1. Measure and calculate the volume of a film canister. Record the volume in a data table like the one shown.

2. Fill the canister with water. Find the mass of the filled canister on the pan balance. Record the value in your data table.

3. Empty the canister of water.

4. Place a few pennies in the canister and put the top on tightly. Find its mass and record the value in your data table.

5. Put the capped film canister into a beaker of water to see if it floats.

6. If it floats, estimate the percentage that is under water. Record this amount in your data table.

7. If it sinks, use the spring scale to measure the apparent weight while it is under water (but not touching the bottom). Record this value in your data table.

8. Repeat steps 4 through 7 using different numbers of pennies for each trial.

9. Calculate the density for each trial in g/cm³.

10. Dispose of the water as instructed by your teacher. Dry wet materials before putting them away.

Data and Observations

Table 1

Volume of canister = _____ cm³

Mass of canister with water = _____ g

Floaters		
Mass with pennies	% below water	Density
Objects with a density less than 1.0 g/cm³ will float in water.		

Sinkers		
Mass with pennies	Apparent weight	Density

---

13 Physics Lab

Analyze and Conclude

1. **Recognizing Spatial Relationships** Look closely at the mass of the floaters and the percentages below the water. What seems to be the rule?

   The density is approximately the same as the percentage of the object that is under water.

   _____

2. **Comparing and Contrasting** Look closely at the sinkers. How much lighter are the canisters when weighed under water?

   Objects that sink seem to weigh less under water. The apparent difference in mass is the same

   as the mass of the water equal to the volume of the object.

   _____

Apply

1. Explain why a steel-hulled boat can float, even though it is quite massive.

   A steel-hulled boat can float if its overall density is less than 1.0 g/cm³. It will sink into the

   water until the weight of the water that is displaced is equal to the weight of the boat.

   _____

2. Icebergs float in salt water (density 1.03 g/cm³) with 1/9 of their volume above water. What is the density of an iceberg?

   If 1/9 is above water, 8/9 is below, so the density of the iceberg is 8/9 that of salt water,

   or 0.92 g/cm³.

13-1

Pocket Lab

Foot Pressure

How much pressure do you exert when standing on the ground with one foot? Is it more or less than air pressure? Estimate your weight in newtons. **Hint:** 500 N = 110 lb. Stand on a piece of paper and have a lab partner trace the outline of your foot. Draw a rectangle that has about the same area as the outline.

Using SI Measurement

Calculate the area of your rectangle in square meters, and use the definition of pressure to estimate your pressure. $P = F/A$.

Sample calculation: $P = F/A$

$= 600.\ N/0.030\ m^2$

$= 2.0 \times 10^4\ Pa$

13-2

Pocket Lab

Floating?

Pour water into a glass or small beaker until it is three-fourths full. Gently place a needle on the surface of the water. Try to float it. Then try to float a paper clip, a metal staple, or a steel razor blade.

Relate Cause and Effect

Explain your results.
The small forces exerted by these objects on the water are not great enough to overcome the intermolecular forces at the surface of the water.

_____

_____

_____

_____

_____

_____

_____

_____

13-3 Pocket Lab

Jumpers

Put on a pair of safety goggles. Examine the jumping disk. Notice that it is slightly curved. Now rub the disk for several seconds until it becomes curved in the other direction. Place the disk on a flat, level surface and stand back.

Make a Hypothesis

Suggest a hypothesis that might explain the jumping. Suggest a method to test your hypothesis. **The disks are bimetallic wafers; they are made of two different metals. Because of heat from your hand, the bottom side expands more than the top side. This differential expansion causes the curvature of the disk to reverse, making the disk jump.**

---

14 Design Your Own Physics Lab

Waves on a Coiled Spring

Problem

How can you model the properties of transverse waves?

Hypothesis

A coiled spring toy can be used to model transverse waves and to investigate wave properties such as speed, frequency, amplitude, and wavelength.

Plan the Experiment

1. Work in pairs or groups, and clear a path of about 6 m for this activity.
2. One member of the team should grip the spring firmly with one hand. Another member of the team should stretch the spring to the length suggested by your teacher. Team members should take turns holding the end of the spring. CAUTION: *Coiled springs easily get out of control. Do not allow them to get tangled or overstretched.*
3. The second team member should then make a quick sideways snap of the wrist to produce transverse wave pulses. Other team members can assist in measuring, timing, and recording data. It is easier to see the motion from one end of the spring, rather than from the side.
4. Design experiments to answer the questions under Analyze and Conclude.
5. **Check the Plan** Make sure your teacher has approved your final plan before you proceed with your experiments.

Possible Materials

a long coiled spring toy
stopwatch
meterstick

Analyze and Conclude

1. **Interpreting Data** What happens to the amplitude of the transverse wave as it travels? **The amplitude (height) of the pulse decreases as it moves along the coiled spring.**

2. **Recognizing Cause and Effect** Does the transverse wave's speed depend upon its amplitude? **No, the pulse takes equal amounts of time to move back and forth along the coiled spring, so the *speed* is *constant*.**

14-1 Pocket Lab

Wave Reflections 🔧 📺

Waves lose amplitude and transfer energy when they reflect from a barrier. What happens to the speed of the waves? Use a wave tank with a projection system. Half-fill the tank with water. Dip your finger into the water near one end of the tank and notice how fast the wave that you make moves to the other end.

Analyze

Does the wave slow down as it travels? Use a stopwatch to measure the time for a wave to cover two lengths, then four lengths, of the wave tank.

No, the time for the wave to travel four lengths is about twice the time for two lengths.

_____

_____

_____

---

14 Physics Lab

3. **Observing and Interpreting** If you put two quick transverse wave pulses into the spring and consider the wavelength to be the distance between the pulses, does the wavelength change as the pulses move?

The pulses stay the same distance apart. The wavelength does not change.

_____

4. **Applying** How can you decrease the wavelength of a transverse wave?

Allowing less time between the pulses makes the wavelength smaller.

_____

5. **Interpreting** As transverse wave pulses travel back and forth on the spring, do they bounce off each other or pass through each other?

The pulses on the coiled spring travel through each other. (This may not be obvious to

students unless they make different sizes or types of pulses.)

Apply

1. How do the speeds of high frequency (short wavelength) transverse waves compare with the speeds of low frequency (long wavelength) transverse waves?

Waves of all frequencies and wavelengths travel at the same speed (in non-dispersive media).

_____

_____

_____

2. Suppose you designed the experiment using longitudinal waves. How would the procedure for longitudinal waves be different from the procedure for transverse waves?

Instead of moving the spring with a sideways snap, the spring would need to be quickly

pulled or pushed along its length.

_____

3. Would you expect the results of an experiment with longitudinal waves to be similar to the results of the transverse wave experiment? Explain why or why not.

Results should be similar. Each movement represents a wave moving through matter, so the

principles remain the same.

14-2

Pocket Lab

Wave Interaction

What happens to the waves coming from different directions when they meet? Do they slow down, bounce off each other, or go through each other?

Design an Experiment

Use a coiled spring toy to test these questions. Record your procedures and observations.

Students can observe that waves go through each other if: (a) they send different amplitude waves

from different directions; (b) one student sends a pressure wave while another student sends a

transverse wave; or (c) one student sends a transverse pulse in a horizontal plane as the other

student makes a similar pulse in a vertical plane.

_____

_____

_____

_____

14-3

Pocket Lab

Bent Out of Shape

What happens to a water wave's speed when the depth of the water changes? How does a change in speed affect the shape of the waves? Try this activity to find out. Use a wave tank with a projection system. Adjust the tank so that the water is shallow on one side and deep on the opposite side. Dip your finger or pencil eraser into the middle of the tank, and gently tap the water to make a circular wave. Watch closely. Do the waves hit the sides of the tank at the same time? What happens to the wavelength in different directions?

Modeling

Make a sketch of the shape of the waves. Label the deep and shallow ends on your drawing. Describe the relationship between the depth of the water and the wave's speed (inverse or direct). What did you notice about the wavelength in different directions?

The wavelength is greater in the deeper water.

_____

_____

15 𝍖 Physics Lab

Speed of Sound

Problem
How can you measure the speed of sound?

Procedure

Materials

tuning fork
hollow glass tube
1000-mL graduated cylinder
hot water
ice water
thermometer
tuning fork hammer
tape measure

1. Place cylinders with hot water on one side of the classroom and ice water on the other side of the classroom.
2. Record the value of the frequency that is stamped on the tuning fork and record the temperature of the water.
3. Wear goggles while using tuning forks next to the glass tubes. With the tube lowered in the cylinder, carefully strike the tuning fork with the rubber hammer.
4. Hold the tuning fork above the glass tube while you slowly raise the tube until the sound is amplified, and is loudest by the tube.
5. Measure L, the distance from the water to the top of the tube, to the nearest 0.5 cm.
6. Trade places with another group on the other side of the room and repeat steps 2–5 using the same tuning fork.
7. Repeat steps 2–6 using a different tuning fork.
8. Dispose of the water as instructed by your teacher. Make sure materials are dry before you put them away.

Data and Observations

Table 1

Hot Water		
Known	$f =$	
Measure	$T =$	$L =$
Calculate	$\lambda =$	$v =$
Cold Water		
Known	$f =$	
Measure	$T =$	$L =$
Calculate	$\lambda =$	$v =$

Students should obtain velocities between 320 m/s and 340 m/s.

---

15 Physics Lab

Analyze and Conclude

1. **Calculating Results** Calculate the values for λ and v.
The velocity should be in the range of 320 m/s to 340 m/s.

2. **Comparing Results** Were the values of v different for cold and hot air? How do the values of v compare for different tuning forks?
Sound seems to travel slightly faster in hot air. The speed of sound increases 0.6 m/s/°C where $v = 331.45$ m/s at 0°C. The value of v shouldn't differ much when using a different tuning fork.

3. **Making Inferences** Write a general statement describing how the speed of sound depends on the variables tested in this experiment.
The speed of sound depends on temperature, with sound having a higher speed the warmer the air is. The speed of sound is independent of frequency.

4. **Forming an Explanation** Describe a possible model of sound moving through air that will explain your results.
The higher the temperature of the air, the more kinetic energy the air molecules have. That is, the air molecules are moving faster and there is less time between collisions. Consequently, they can transmit a sound wave quicker.

Apply

1. What would an orchestra sound like if the higher frequencies traveled faster than the lower frequencies?
A person in the back of the auditorium would hear the high notes before the low notes.

15-1

Pocket Lab

Sound Off

Take a meterstick and tape recorder to the band room. Measure the entire length of a wind instrument. Ask a musician to play the lowest note possible on her instrument. Make a recording of the lowest note. Return to the physics room.

Analyze and Conclude

For the lowest note, $L = \lambda/2$, what is the wavelength played by the instrument? Use this estimate of the wavelength and the wave equation to predict the frequency. **Hint:** $v = \lambda f$. Use a frequency generator to try to match the recorded note. Read the value on the frequency generator. Is this reading close to your prediction?

Student comparison of calculated frequencies to values on the frequency generator should be

within 25%.

_____

_____

_____

_____

_____

15-2

Pocket Lab

Ring, Ring

How good is your hearing? Here is a simple test to find out. Find a penny, a nickel, a dime, and a quarter. Ask a lab partner to drop them in any order and listen closely. Can you identify the sound of each coin with your eyes closed?

Analyze and Conclude

Describe the differences in the sounds. What are the physical factors that cause the differences in the sounds? Can you suggest any patterns?

The natural frequency of any object depends on its geometry, its material, and its size.

Smaller and thinner objects vibrate faster!

_____

_____

_____

_____

_____

_____

_____

16 〰 Physics Lab

Light Ray Paths

Problem

How do light waves travel?

Materials

4 unlined index cards (4 × 6)

clay

40-watt lightbulb (nonfrosted) in a fixture

4–6 flat mirrors, approximately 10 cm × 15 cm

medium nail

ruler

Procedure

1. Draw two diagonals on each index cards, using the ruler. Mark the center of each card.

2. Punch the center of three of the cards with the nail.

3. Stand one of the punched cards so that its longer edge is parallel to a desk or tabletop. Use two pea-sized lumps of clay to secure the card to the table.

4. Stand the remaining cards on the table so they are about 10 cm apart. Place the card without the hole last. Use clay to secure all the cards.

5. Arrange the cards so their outside edges are in a straight line. Use the ruler to check the alignment. Once your setup is complete, dim the room lights.

6. Ask your partner to hold the light fixture so the light shines through the hole in the first card.

7. Check the alignment of the two other punched cards so you can see the light shining on the fourth card.

8. Place a mirror in front of the fourth card so the light shines on it. Give each person in your group a mirror, and have them hold it in a position that reflects the light beam to the next person's mirror. Be careful not to reflect the light beam into someone's eye.

9. When you have completed the lab, recycle the index cards and save the clay for use again.

Data and Observations

1. Decide how to place the mirrors so that you can reflect the light onto the back of the card without the hole.
Most students will recognize that the fourth card and the mirrors need to be placed at the vertices of a closed polygon.

2. Draw a diagram showing your mirror setup. Use arrows to mark the path of light between the mirrors and the card.
Student diagrams should indicate that light travels in straight paths.

---

16 Physics Lab

3. Describe how the brightness of the light shining on the first mirror compares with the brightness of the light reflected from the last mirror.
Students will likely observe that the brightness of the light beam diminishes as it is reflected from one mirror to the next.

Analyze and Conclude

1. **Analyzing Data** How can you describe the path of light from one mirror to the next?
The light travels in a straight line.

2. **Critical Thinking** What explanation can you give for your observations concerning the relative brightness of the reflections?
Even though the light passes through three nail holes, the light rays are not parallel. This causes them to continue to spread out after each reflection. Since the same amount of light energy covers a greater area as it strikes the next mirror, the light intensity decreases with each reflection. Also, there is no mirror with 100% reflectance, so light intensity is lost just through reflection as well.

Apply

1. Use your observations to draw a diagram showing how a shadow forms.
Student drawings should indicate that light travels from a source to an object. The rays stop where the object is solid, forming a shadow. The rays continue if they are not blocked by the object.

16-1 Pocket Lab

An Illuminating Matter

Which is more efficient, or has the highest lm/W, a lower- or higher-power lightbulb? To find out, look at your lightbulbs at home and record the power and lumens for at least three different bulbs.

Graph Your Results

Make a graph of power (horizontal axis) versus lumens (vertical axis). Summarize your results.

Higher-wattage bulbs are more efficient.

_____
_____
_____
_____
_____
_____

16-2 Pocket Lab

Hot and Cool Colors

Some artists refer to red and orange as hot colors and green and blue as cool colors. But does emitting red or orange light really indicate that an object is hotter than one emitting blue or green? Try this to find out. Obtain a pair of prism glasses or a piece of diffraction grating from your teacher. Find a lamp with a dimmer switch and turn off the light. Next, slowly turn the dimmer so that the light gets brighter and brighter. To get the best effect, turn off all the other lights in the room.

Analyze and Conclude

Which colors appeared first when the light was dim? Which colors were the last to appear? How do these colors relate to the temperature of the filament?

When the filament is cool, you will see reds and oranges. The blues and violets will not be seen

until the filament reaches a higher temperature.

_____
_____
_____
_____
_____
_____

Date _____ Period _____ Name _____

16-3

Pocket Lab

Soap Solutions

Dip a ring into soap solution and hold it at a 45° angle to the horizontal. Look for color bands to form in horizontal stripes.

Analyze and Conclude

Why do the bands move? Why are the bands horizontal? What type of pattern would you see if you looked through the soap with a red filter? Try it. Describe and explain your results. **Students looking through a red filter will see alternating red and dark bands. The lines move downward because the soap is thinning at the top. Students looking through a red filter will see alternating red and dark bands.**

_____

_____

_____

_____

_____

_____

_____

Date _____ Period _____ Name _____

16-4

Pocket Lab

Light Polarization

Obtain a polarizing filter from your teacher to take home. Look through the filter at various objects as you rotate the filter. Make a record of those objects that seem to change in brightness as the filter is rotated.

Recognize Cause and Effect

What seems to be the pattern? **Students should notice that the contrast between clouds and the sky is greatly changed as the polarizer is rotated. Smooth reflecting surfaces such as windows and car windshields will have changed noticeably.**

_____

_____

_____

Date _____ Period _____ Name _____

17 〰 Physics Lab

Bending of Light

Problem
How is the index of refraction of light in water determined?

Procedure

Part I

1. Draw a line dividing the graph paper in half.
2. Use the felt-tip pen to draw a vertical line at the center of the straight edge of the plastic dish. This line will be your object.
3. Place the edge of the dish along the straight line so that the dish is on the bottom half of the paper. Trace the outline of the dish on the paper.
4. Mark the position of the object on your paper.
5. Add water until the dish is three-fourths full.
6. Lay a ruler on the bottom half of the paper. Adjust the position until the edge of the ruler seems to point at the object when you look through the water.
7. Have a lab partner check to verify that the ruler position is accurate.
8. Draw a line along the ruler edge to the edge of the dish.
9. Repeat steps 6–8 for a different position of the ruler.

Part II

1. Wipe the vertical line from the dish and draw a vertical line at the center of the curved edge. This is your new object.
2. Repeat all steps from Part I, but this time sight the ruler on the top half of the paper.
3. Dispose of the water as instructed by your teacher. Dry and put away materials that can be reused.

Data and Observations

1. Look at the sight lines you drew in Part I. Did the light bend when moving from water to air?
   The sight lines point directly at the object. The light did not bend when passing from water into air.

2. For Part II, do the sight lines point directly toward the object?
   The sight lines do not point directly toward the object.

Materials
graph paper
felt-tip pen
ruler
semicircular plastic dish
water

Name _____

17 Physics Lab

3. For Part II, draw a line from the object position to the point where each sight line touches the dish.
   Drawing these lines emphasizes that light bends at the boundary.
4. Draw the normal at each point where the sight line touched the dish.
   The angles must always be measured from the normal.
5. Measure the angles from the normal for the angles in air and water.
   The angles in the air will be larger than angles in water.

Analyze and Conclude

1. **Interpreting Data** Explain why the light did not bend in Part I. (Hint: Draw the normal to the surface.)
   In Part 1, the light passed directly along the normal. Whenever light passes along the normal, it does not bend.

2. **Calculating Values** Calculate *n*, using Snell's law.
   Student values should be in the range of 1.2 to 1.45 (10% error).

Apply

1. Could a flat piece of material be used for focusing light? Make a drawing to support your answer. **Make a drawing to support your answer. A flat piece of material would not focus light. All the light rays refract in the same direction when passing through it.**

Physics: Principles and Problems

Physics Lab and Pocket Lab Worksheets 85

86 Physics Lab and Pocket Lab Worksheets

Physics: Principles and Problems

40T Teacher Guide and Answers

Physics: Principles and Problems

17-1

Pocket Lab

Reflections

Toss a tennis ball or a handball against a wall so that it will bounce to a lab partner, but first predict where the ball must hit on the wall to bounce in the right direction. If your partner moves closer (or farther) from the wall, does your rule still work?

Compare and Contrast

Write a general rule that seems to work. Does your rule for the bouncing ball work for predicting the path of light? How is it similar? **This rule can be applied to light as long as the reflecting surface is smooth.**

_____

_____

_____

_____

_____

17-2

Pocket Lab

Refraction

Place a small hexagonal nut in the center of the bottom of a 1000-mL beaker. Pour water into the beaker until it is half full of water. Look through the sides of the beaker at the nut while placing a ruler along the tabletop so that the edge of the ruler appears to point to the center of the nut. Do you think that the ruler really points to the nut? Look from the top to see where the ruler points. Place a golf ball on the nut. Look through the sides of the beaker at the ball and adjust the edge of the ruler to point to the edge of the ball. Look from the top.

Analyze and Conclude

Describe your observations. Make a drawing to show why the ball appears to be so wide. **Students may be surprised to find that the edge of the ruler points to the center of the nut. The light that moves along the center of curvature does not bend. This light moves perpendicular to the curved surface. The golf ball appears wider, but not taller. The light bends because it does not hit perpendicular to the surface.**

_____

_____

_____

17-3 Pocket Lab

Cool Images

CAUTION: *Avoid staring directly into the laser beam or at bright reflections.*

Can you light an electric bulb without any electrical connection and can you make the image of the bulb in a mirror glow? Try this activity to find out. Place a 100-watt bulb in an electric socket but do not turn on the electricity. Place this next to a mirror. Sit so that you can see both the bulb and its reflection. Aim a penlight laser at the bulb.

Observe and Infer

Did you notice that the bulb glowed red and that the image also glowed? What would happen if you aimed the laser at the image? Try it. Use a ray diagram to explain your results.

When the laser is aimed at a mirror where the bulb's image had been, the laser beam will reflect

back onto the bulb itself. The bulb gains energy from the waves emitted by the laser. Again, the

bulb and the image(s) will glow red!

_____

_____

17-4 Pocket Lab

Personal Rainbow

You can make your own personal rainbow when the sun is out and low in the sky for easier viewing. Adjust a garden hose to produce a gentle spray. Face away from the sun so that you can see your shadow. Spray the water upwards above your shadow and watch closely until you see the colors. By moving the spray in an arc from side to side, you will produce your own personal rainbow.

Analyze and Conclude

Did you notice the order of the colors in the spectrum of visible lights? Could you easily see each of the colors ROYGBIV? Which color was on the inside edge? Which color was on the outside edge?

Although the spectrum can be seen, it will be extremely difficult to see the boundaries between the

different colors. Violet should be on the inside edge, but most students will see the blue because

the eye is more sensitive to blue than violet. Red and orange will be the colors on the outside.

_____

_____

_____

_____

_____

18 ⟨⟨⟨ Physics Lab

Seeing Is Believing

Problem
How can you locate the image of a lens?

Materials
large-diameter convex lens

large-diameter concave lens

2 small balls of clay

2 rulers

2- or 3-cm-long nail

2 pieces of paper

Procedure
1. Assemble the equipment as shown in your text on p. 433 using the concave lens.
2. Look through the lens to make sure that you can see both ends of the nail. Move the nail closer or farther from the lens until both ends are visible.

Data and Observations
1. Mark the paper to show the tip of the nail, the head of the nail, and also the lens line.
2. Line up your straight edge to point to the head of the nail. Have your lab partner verify that the edge is accurate.
3. Draw the line of sight.
4. Move to another position and draw a second line of sight to the head of the nail.
5. Repeat steps 2–4, this time drawing two lines of sight to the tip of the nail.
6. Use a new sheet of paper and repeat steps 1–5 using the convex lens.
7. When you are finished, put away any materials that can be reused.

Analyze And Conclude
1. **Analyzing Data** The image position can be located by extending lines of sight until they intersect. Extend the two lines of sight that point to the image head. Extend the two lines of sight that point to the image tip. Describe the results.
The lines of sight show that the image of the nail is smaller than the nail, and also that the image is closer to the lens than the nail.

---

2. **Analyzing Data** Repeat the analysis for the convex lens, and describe the results.
The lines of sight show that the image of the nail is larger than the nail and is farther away from the lens than the nail.

3. **Comparing Data** Record your observations and image descriptions in a table.

Table 1

Lens	Image Size (with respect to object)	Image Type (upright or upside down)	Image Location (with respect to object and lens)
concave			
convex			

Results vary with the object's position in relation to the focal point of the lens.

4. **Extending Results** How would the image size and location change if you moved the object closer to the lens? Do the answers depend on whether the lens is concave or convex?
concave: larger and closer

convex: smaller and closer

Apply
1. Describe an application of a similar arrangement for a convex lens.
A single converging lens is often used as a magnifying glass. This lens produces an image that is larger and farther away than the object.

18-1

Pocket Lab

Where's the image?

Suppose that you are standing directly in front of a mirror and see your image. Exactly where is the image? Here is a way to find out. Find a camera with a focusing ring that has distances marked on it. Stand 1.0 m from a mirror and focus on the edge of the mirror. Check the reading on the focusing ring. It should be 1.0 m. Now focus on your image. What is the reading on the ring now?

Analyze and Conclude

Summarize your results and write a brief conclusion.

When the image is in focus, the reading on the ring will be 2.0 m.

18-2

Pocket Lab

Real or Virtual?

Hold a small concave mirror at arm's length and look at your image. What do you see? Is the image in front or behind the mirror? What happens to the image as you slowly bring the mirror toward your face?

Analyze and Conclude

Briefly summarize your observations and conclusions.

When the object is closer to the mirror than the focal point, the image is virtual, erect, and enlarged.

18-3

Pocket Lab

Focal Points

Take a concave mirror into an area of direct sunlight. Use a piece of clay to hold the mirror steady so that the concave mirror directly faces the sun. Move your finger toward or away from the mirror in the area of reflected light to find the brightest spot (focal point). Turn the mirror so that the convex side faces the sun and repeat the experiment.

Analyze and Conclude

Record and explain your results.

It is important that students understand why there is no focal point on the convex side.

The reflected light is diverging.

18-4

Pocket Lab

Makeup

Do you have a makeup mirror in your home? Does this mirror produce images that are larger or smaller than your face? What does this tell you about the curvature? Feel the surface of the mirror. Does this confirm your prediction about the curvature? Try to discover the focal length of this mirror.

Analyze and Conclude

Record your procedure and briefly explain your observations and results.

The image of a face is enlarged. The curvature is concave. It is possible to feel the concave

curvature on most makeup mirrors. Students might use sunlight to find the focal point, but they will

not be able to produce high-quality images.

18-5

Pocket Lab

Burned Up

Convex (converging) lenses can be used as magnifying glasses. Use someone's eyeglasses to see if they magnify. Are the glasses converging? Can the lenses be used in sunlight to start a fire?

Analyze and Conclude

Use your answers to describe the lenses.

The surface area of the lenses cannot gather enough energy to start a fire.

18-6

Pocket Lab

Fish-Eye Lens

How can fish focus light with their eyes? The light from an object in the water goes from the water into the fish eye, which is also mostly water. Obtain a converging lens and observe that it can be used as a magnifying glass. Now hold the lens under water in an aquarium. Does the lens still magnify?

Analyze and Conclude

Compare the magnifying ability of the glass lens when used under water and in air. Would a more curved lens bend the light more? Would you predict that the index of refraction of the material in a fish eye is the same as water? Defend your prediction.

To be effective, the fish eye must be more curved and also have an index of refraction greater than

that of water.

18-7 Pocket Lab

Bright Ideas

Stick the edge of a converging lens into a ball of clay and place the lens on a tabletop. Use a small light-bulb on one side and a screen on the other side to get a sharp image of the bulb. Predict what will happen to the image if you place your hand over the top half of the lens. Try it.

Analyze and Conclude

What happened? How much of the lens is needed for a complete image?

A complete image is formed even when only a small portion of the lens is uncovered.

_____

_____

_____

_____

_____

---

19 Physics Lab

Wavelengths of Colors

Problem

How can you accurately measure the wavelength of four colors of light?

Procedure

1. Cut the index card lengthwise into four equal strips.
2. Write the letters "O" (orange), "Y" (yellow), "G" (green), and "B" (blue) on the strips.
3. Place the ball of clay 1.0 m on the bench in front of the lamp. Use the ball of clay to support the diffraction grating.
4. Plug in the lamp and turn off the room lights.
5. When you look through the diffraction grating, you should see bands of colors to the sides of the bulb. If you do not see the colors to the sides, then rotate the diffraction grating 90° until you do.
6. Have a lab partner stand behind the lamp and move the strip labeled "O" from side to side until you see it in place with the middle of its color. Ask your partner to tape the strip to the table at that point.
7. Repeat step 6 for each of the other colored strips.
8. When you are completely finished with the lab, dispose or recycle appropriate materials. Put away materials that can be reused.

Materials

meterstick
index card
40-W straight filament light
ball of clay
tape
diffraction grating

Data and Observations

Table 1

Color	x	d	L	λ
Students will observe and record the four colors of light in the interference pattern produced by the diffraction grating. Here are typical values from the lab:				

Color	Wavelength
orange	600 nm
yellow	580 nm
green	530 nm
blue	420 nm

(Student values are usually within 5% of these.)

19-1

Pocket Lab

Hot Lights

Plug a 100-W clear lamp into a Variac (variable power supply). Turn off the room lights. Look through a diffraction grating at the lamp as you slowly increase the power.

Observing and Inferring

Describe what you see. Which color appears first? What happens to the brightness of previous colors as new colors become visible? What is the order of the colors?

All colors will get brighter as the temperature of the lamp filament increases. Red and orange will

occur at lower temperatures. Other colors will be added in the order of the spectrum.

_____

_____

_____

_____

_____

_____

_____

_____

_____

---

19 Physics Lab

Analyze and Conclude

1. Observing and Inferring What color is closest to the lamp? Suggest a reason and list the order that colors occur, beginning from red.

The violet light appears closest to the bulb. This occurs because violet has the shortest

wavelength.

_____

_____

2. Making and Using a Table Use a data table or a spreadsheet to record x, d, and L for each of the four colors. Measure and record x for each strip to the nearest 0.1 cm. Record the value of d provided by your teacher.

Assess individual student data tables for reasonable answers.

3. Calculating Use the equation $\lambda = xd/L$ to calculate the wavelength for each color and record this value in nanometers in your data table or spreadsheet.

Assess individual student data tables for reasonable answers.

Apply

1. How could diffraction gratings be used in conjunction with telescopes?

Astronomers measure wavelengths of light emitted from stars to identify the elements

producing the light.

_____

_____

2. Suppose your diffraction grating had more grooves per centimeter. How would this change the diffraction pattern you see?

More grooves per centimeter would make the distance between the grooves (d) less. This

would cause the interference patterns to spread out more.

_____

19-2

Pocket Lab

Laser Spots

Turn on a laser so that it makes a spot on the center of a movie screen. What would you expect to happen to the spot if you were to put a piece of window screening in the pathway of the beam? Explain your prediction.

Observing and Interpreting

What really happened? Use the wave theory to explain your results.

Light is behaving like a wave. The light striking the edges of the screen forms an interference pattern when it combines on the movie screen.

_____
_____
_____
_____
_____
_____
_____
_____

19-3

Pocket Lab

Lights in the Night

Obtain small pieces of red and blue cellophane. When it is dark, find a long stretch of road and estimate the distance to cars when you can just barely tell that they have two headlights on. When a car is far away, its lights blend together. Look at these distant lights through the red cellophane and also through the blue cellophane. Which color makes it easier to resolve the two lights into separate images?

Determining Cause and Effect

Explain why one color is more effective in separating the lights. Suggest how the use of blue filters might be useful for scientists working with telescopes or microscopes.

Blue light is more effective because its diffraction pattern is narrower than that of red light.

Scientists could use blue filters to increase the resolving power of microscopes and telescopes, thereby seeing small and distant objects more distinctly.

_____
_____
_____
_____
_____
_____
_____
_____
_____

20 Physics Lab

What's the charge?

Problem

Can you see the effects of electrostatic charging? How can you increase the amount of charge on an object without discharging it?

Materials

- 30 cm × 30 cm block of polystyrene
- 22-cm aluminum pie pan
- plastic cup
- drinking straw
- wool
- transparent tape
- thread
- pith ball (or small piece of plastic foam packing material)
- liquid graphite

Procedure

1. Paint the pith ball with graphite and allow it to dry.
2. Tape the inverted cup to the aluminum pie pan. Secure the straw to the top of the cup and use the thread to attach the ball as shown in your textbook on page 467.
3. Rub the foam with wool, then remove the wool.
4. Holding onto the plastic cup, lower the pie pan until it is about 3 cm above the foam block and then slowly lift it away.
5. Place the pie pan directly on the charged foam block and lift it away.
6. Bring your finger near the ball until they touch.
7. Place the pie pan on the foam block and touch the edge of the pie pan with your finger. Then remove the pie pan from the foam block and touch the ball again with your finger.
8. Repeat step 7 several times without recharging the foam block.
9. When finished, recycle or dispose of appropriate materials. Put away materials that can be reused.

Data and Observations

Table 1

Description of Event	Observations

---

20 Physics Lab

Analyze and Conclude

1. **Forming a Description** As the pie pan was brought near the charged block, could you detect a force between the neutral pie pan and the charged foam block? Describe it.
A definite pulling force was felt. The force increased as the distance decreased.

2. **Interpreting Observations** Explain what happened to the ball in step 4 and step 5.
In step 4, the small ball swung away from the edge of the plate, but as the plate was raised, the ball returned to its former position. In step 5, the ball swung farther from the plate. The ball stayed away from the edge even when the plate was lifted from the foam.

3. **Analyzing Results** Make a drawing to show the distribution of charges on the neutral pie pan as it is lowered toward the charged foam block.
The negative charge on the polystyrene pushes electrons on the plate so the bottom of the plate is slightly positive and the top of the plate is slightly negative.

4. **Inferring Relationships** What was the reason for using the ball on a thread? Explain the back-and-forth motion of the ball in step 6.
The pith ball is a sensitive indicator that shows when the edge of the plate is charged. Each time the ball touches the pie pan, it removes some electrons. These electrons are deposited on your finger. This process repeats.

5. **Interpreting Observations** Does the polystyrene block seem to run out of charges in step 8?
A strong spark will be made several times. The spark does not seem to lessen in intensity. The foam does not "run out" of charges.

Apply

1. Clear plastic wrap is sold to seal up containers of food. Suggest a reason why it clings to itself.
The plastic wrap is a good insulator. Excess charges on the wrap probably induce opposite charges on adjacent layers.

Date _____ Period _____ Name _____

20-1

Pocket Lab

Charged Up

Rub a balloon with wool. Touch the balloon to the knob of an electroscope and watch the leaves.

Analyze and Conclude

Describe the result. Make a drawing to explain the result. Touch the knob of the electroscope to make the leaves fall. Would you expect that the wool could move the leaves? Why? Try it. Explain your results. **The balloon becomes charged when it is rubbed, as does the wool. When both the balloon and the wool are touched to the electroscope, the leaves spread.**

_____

_____

_____

_____

_____

_____

Date _____ Period _____ Name _____

20-2

Pocket Lab

Reach Out

Start with the leaves of an electroscope down. Predict what should happen if you bring a charged balloon near (but not touching) the top of the electroscope.

Analyze and Conclude

Explain your prediction. Try it. Describe and explain your results. **This occurs because the charges in the balloon push some of the like charges away from the knob of the electroscope and into the leaves. Thus, the leaves have a temporary charge.**

_____

_____

_____

_____

_____

21 Physics Lab

Charges, Energy, and Voltage

Problem

How can you make a model that demonstrates the relationship of charge, energy, and voltage?

Materials

ball of clay
ruler
cellophane tape
12 steel balls, 3-mm diameter
paper

Procedure

1. Use the clay to support the ruler vertically on the tabletop. The 0 end should be at the table.
2. Cut a 2 cm × 8 cm rectangular piece of paper and write on it "3 V = 3 J/C."
3. Cut three more rectangles and label them: 6 V = 6 J/C, 9 V = 9 J/C, and 12 V = 12 J/C.
4. Tape the 3-V rectangle to the 3" mark on the ruler, the 6-V to the 6" mark, and so on.
5. Let each steel ball represent 1 C of charge.
6. Lift and tape four steel balls to the 3-V rectangle, three to the 6-V rectangle, and so on.
7. When you are completely finished with the lab, dispose of or recycle appropriate materials. Put away materials that can be reused.

Data and Observations

1. Review the data table below.

Table 1

Level	Charge	Voltage	Energy
	4	3	12
	3	6	18
	2	9	18
	1	12	12

2. Fill in the data table for your model for each level of the model.
3. The model shows different amounts of charges at different energy levels. Where should steel balls be placed to show a zero energy level? Explain.
The steel balls on the tabletop are at zero energy level. This is the "0" on the ruler.

---

21 Physics Lab

Analyze and Conclude

1. **Analyzing Data** How much energy is required to lift each coulomb of charge from the tabletop to the 9-V level?
Each coulomb of charge requires 9 J to lift it to the 9-V level.

2. **Analyzing Data** What is the total potential energy stored in the 9-V level?
Each coulomb of charge has 9 J of potential energy. The total energy stored at the 9-V level is
2×9 J = 18 J.

3. **Relating Concepts** The total energy of the charges in the 6-V level is not 6 J. Explain this.
The energy at the 6-V level is 3 C × 6 J/C = 18 J.

4. **Making Predictions** How much energy would be given off if the charges in the 9-V level fell to the 6-V level? Explain.
The change in energy would be 2 C × –3 J/C = –6 J.

Apply

1. A 9-V battery is very small. A 12-V car battery is very big. Use your model to help explain why two 9-V batteries will not start your car.
It takes energy to start the car. The energy is the voltage times the number of charges with stored energy. The amount of charge stored in one or even two 9-V batteries is too small. The 12-V car battery has considerably more charges and therefore a lot more stored energy.

21-1 Pocket Lab

Electric Fields

How does the electric field around a charged piece of plastic foam vary in strength and direction? Try this activity to find out. Tie a pith ball on the end of a 20-cm nylon thread and tie the other end to a plastic straw. When you hold the straw horizontally, notice that the ball hangs straight down on the thread. Now rub a piece of wool on a 30 cm × 30 cm square of plastic foam to charge both objects. Stand the foam in a vertical orientation. Hold the straw and touch the pith ball to the wool, then slowly bring the hanging ball towards the charged plastic foam. Move the pith ball to different regions and notice the angle of the thread.

Analyze and Conclude

Why did the ball swing toward the charged plastic? Explain in terms of the electric field. Did the angle of the thread change? Why? Does the angle of the thread indicate the direction of the electric field? Explain.

The field is strongest near the center of the foam, and the field gets stronger as the distance separating the foam and the ball gets smaller.

_____

_____

_____

_____

_____

---

22 Physics Lab

Mystery Cans

Problem

An electric device is inside each film can. How can you design and build a circuit to determine whether the resistance is constant for different voltages?

Procedure

1. Identify the variables to be measured.

2. Design your circuit and label each component. Use the proper symbols to make your drawing of the setup. Show your teacher your plan before proceeding further.

3. Build the circuit of your design and slowly increase the voltage on your power supply to make sure that your meters are working properly. Do not exceed one amp or the current limitation set by your teacher. Reverse connections as needed.

4. Make at least three measurements of voltage and current for each can.

5. When you have completed the lab, put away materials that can be reused. Dispose of or recycle materials as appropriate.

Materials

power supply with variable voltage
wires with clips
multimeter
ammeter
3 film cans for each group

Data and Observations

1. Make a data table with at least three places for measurements on each can.

Table 1

Trial	V	I	R
Can 1			
Can 2			
Can 3			

22 Physics Lab

Name _____

Analyze and Conclude

1. **Calculating Results** Calculate R for each test.
The calculated ratio should be constant for two of the resistor cans, but students will discover that the resistance of the mini lamp will increase as the voltage is increased.

2. **Graphing Data** Graph V versus I for all of your data. If possible, use a graphing calculator or computer plotting program. Draw a separate line for each can. Identify the relationship between variables.
The data lines for the resistors will have a fairly constant slope, but the data line for the mini lamp will be increasing.

3. **Interpreting Graphs** Determine the slope for each of your lines.
The graph shows that the carbon resistors have a constant resistance, but the mini lamp resistance increases with voltage.

4. **Comparing Values** Open each can to see the marked values of the resistors. Compare your predicted values to the actual values.
Students who took reasonable care to read the meters carefully should be within a few percentage points for the resistor values.

22 Physics Lab

Name _____

Apply

1. Most incandescent lamps burn out when they are switched on rather than when they have been on for a while. Predict what happens to the resistance and the current when a cold lamp is switched on. Make a graph of R versus t and also I versus t for the first few seconds. Calculate the resistance of an operating 60-W lamp at 120 V. Now use a multimeter as an ohmmeter to measure the resistance of a cold 60-W lamp. Describe your results.
The resistance of a cold lamp is lower than that of a hot lamp. The operating resistance of the 100-watt lamp is 144 ohms, but a measurement of a cold 100-watt lamp is only about 12 ohms.

22-1

Pocket Lab

Lighting Up 🔦 ✍

Use a D cell and a 10-cm length of wire to light a miniature lamp. Make a sketch of two circuits that work and two circuits that do not work.

Analyze and Conclude

Can you light the lamp without having two connecting points on the lamp? Does a lamp connected in your house have two connecting points? Suggest a reason why two are needed. **A continuous path from cell to lamp to cell is needed for success. Even in a household lamp, two connections are required. (The electrical cord contains two separate wires.)**

22-2

Pocket Lab

Running Out 🔦 ✍

Use the proper symbols and design a drawing that shows a power supply in a continuous circuit with two miniature lamps. Next, draw the circuit with an ammeter included to measure the electrical flow between the power supply and the bulbs. Make a third drawing to show the ammeter at a position to measure the electrical flow between the bulbs.

Test Your Prediction

Would you predict the current between the lamps to be more or less than the current before the lamps? Why? Build the circuits to find out. Record your results. **The drawing can be used to help set up the actual equipment.**

_____
_____
_____
_____
_____
_____
_____

22-4 Pocket Lab

Heating Up

Look at the markings on three resistors. Predict which resistor would allow the most current through it using a constant voltage. Under the same conditions, predict which resistor will heat the most. Explain your prediction.

The lowest-value resistor will allow the most current and heat up the fastest.

_____

_____

_____

_____

Test Your Predictions

Tape a thermometer bulb to the resistor. Turn on the power for one minute. Measure the temperature. Allow the resistor to cool off and then repeat the procedure with the remaining two resistors.

CAUTION: Do not touch the resistors with power supplied. They may be extremely hot. Wait two minutes after turning off the power to remove the thermometer.

22-3 Pocket Lab

Appliances

Look closely at three electric appliances in your home. Record the power (watts) or the current (amps) of each appliance. Assume that each appliance operates at 120 V. Determine the resistance of each appliance.

Analyze and Conclude

Relate the power used in an appliance to its resistance.

Appliances with small resistances (such as toasters or hair dryers) have large power ratings.

_____

_____

_____

_____

23

Design Your Own
Physics Lab

Circuits

Problem

Suppose that three identical lamps are connected to the same power supply. Can a circuit be made such that one lamp is brighter than the others and stays on if either of the others is loosened in its socket?

Hypothesis

One lamp should be brighter than the other two and remain at the same brightness when either of the other two lamps is loosened in its socket so that it goes out.

Plan the Experiment

1. Sketch a series circuit and predict the relative brightness of each lamp. Predict what would happen to the other lamps when one is loosened so that it goes out.

2. Sketch a parallel circuit and predict the relative brightness of each lamp. Predict what would happen to the other lamps when one is loosened so that it goes out.

3. Draw a combination circuit. Label the lamps A, B, and C. Would the bulbs have the same brightness? Predict what would happen to the other two lamps when each lamp in turn is loosened so that it goes out.

4. **Check the Plan** Show your circuits and predictions to your teacher before starting to build the circuits.

5. When you have completed the lab, dispose of or recycle appropriate materials. Put away materials that can be reused.

Analyze and Conclude

1. **Interpreting Data** Did the series circuit meet the requirements? Explain.

   No. The three lamps go on and off together and have the same brightness.

2. **Interpreting Data** Did the parallel circuit meet either of the requirements? Explain.

   The lamps can be turned on and off individually, but they all have the same brightness.

Possible Materials

power supply with variable voltage
wires with clips
3 identical lamps and sockets

---

23 Physics Lab

3. **Formulating Hypotheses** Explain the circuit that solved the problem in terms of current.

   The correct circuit has two parallel branches. One branch contains only one lamp that is brighter than the other two. The other parallel branch has two dimmer lamps in series.

   Loosening either of these lamps will turn off the other dim lamp, but will not affect the flow through the bright lamp.

4. **Formulating Hypotheses** Use the definition of *resistance* to explain why one lamp was brighter and the other two were equally dim.

   The lamp in its own branch had the full voltage of the power supply. The two dim lamps each had half the voltage of the power supply. Because the two dim lamps in series with each other have more resistance, the current through these lamps is less than through the bright lamp.

5. **Making Predictions** Predict how the voltages would compare when measured across each lamp in the correct circuit.

   Assuming that the power supply is at 6.0 V, the bright lamp will be measured at 6.0 V and each dim lamp will be at 3.0 V.

6. **Testing Conclusions** Use a voltmeter to check your prediction.

   Measurements should verify the predictions.

Apply

1. Can one wall switch control several lights in the same room? Are the lamps in parallel or series? Are the switches in parallel or series with the lamps? Explain.

   One wall switch can control many overhead lights. The lamps are in parallel with each other, but the switch is in series with the lamps. Opening the switch stops the electrical flow through all of the overhead lamps.

23-1

Pocket Lab

Series Resistance

Hook up a power supply, a resistor, and an ammeter in a series circuit. Predict what will happen to the current in the circuit when a second, identical resistor is added in series to the circuit. Predict the new currents when the circuit contains three and four resistors in series. Explain your prediction. Try it.

_____

_____

_____

Analyze and Conclude

Make a data table to show your results. Briefly explain your results. (**Hint:** Include the idea of resistance.)
The current is inversely proportional to the number of resistors.

_____

_____

_____

23-2

Pocket Lab

Parallel Resistance

Hook up a power supply, a resistor, and an ammeter in a series circuit. Predict what will happen to the current in the circuit when a second, identical resistor is added in parallel to the first. Predict the new currents when the circuit contains three and four resistors in parallel. Explain your prediction. Try it.

_____

_____

_____

Analyze and Conclude

Make a data table to show your results. Briefly explain your results. (**Hint:** Include the idea of resistance.)
The resistance decreases with the addition of more parallel branches.

_____

_____

_____

23-3 Pocket Lab

Ammeter Resistance

Design an experiment using a power supply, a voltmeter, an ammeter, a resistor, and some wires to determine the resistance of the ammeter. Make a sketch of your setup and include measurements and equations.

Communicating Results

What is the resistance of the ammeter? Be prepared to present your experiment to the class.
The reading on the voltmeter should be very low because of the low resistance of the ammeter.

---

24 Design Your Own Physics Lab

Coils and Currents

Problem

You have seen that an electric current affects a magnetic compass needle. What happens to pieces of iron located inside a coil that carries a current? What is the effect of changing the magnitude of the current? Does an alternating current produce a different effect from that of a direct current?

Hypothesis

Write a testable hypothesis that addresses the questions posed in the problem.

Most students will suggest that magnetic field strength and its effects will increase as the current increases. Students may be unsure about the magnetic field for AC circuits.

Possible Materials

a ring stand with crossbar and clamp

two 20-cm lengths of thick, insulated iron wire

75 cm of thread

magnetic compass

miniature lamp with socket

500-turn, aircore solenoid

a variable power supply that can produce AC and DC voltages and currents

electrical leads and alligator clips

Plan the Experiment

1. Develop a plan and design a circuit you can use to test your hypothesis.

2. **Check the Plan** Show your teacher your plan before you start to build the circuit. CAUTION: *Be sure the power supply is off as you build the circuit.*

3. CAUTION: *Your teacher must inspect your setup before you turn the power on and begin your investigation.*

4. When you have completed the lab, dispose of or recycle appropriate materials. Put away materials that can be reused.

Analyze and Conclude

1. **Making Observations** Describe your observations as you increased the direct current produced by the power supply.
The hanging wires moved farther away from each other. The magnetic field of the coil magnetized them.

24 Physics Lab

Name _____

2. Drawing Conclusions What conclusion can you make regarding the strength of the magnetic field as you increased the current?

The magnetic field became stronger as the current was increased. The wires moved further

apart.

3. Interpreting Results What can you conclude from the results of your experimentation comparing the effects of direct and alternating currents?

As the alternating current changed direction, so did the magnetic field in the coil and the

polarities of the hanging wires. The compass didn't show any change because the reversals

were quick.

4. Making Predictions Predict what would happen to the magnetic field if the number of turns on the coil was doubled. How would you test your prediction?

The strength of the magnetic field would increase. Students might suggest repeating the

experiment with a coil having twice the number of turns. They might hypothesize that the

hanging wires would move farther apart, indicating a stronger field.

Apply

1. Large and powerful electromagnets are often used at scrap metal facilities. Would you expect that these magnets use AC current or DC current? Explain why.

Running a DC current through an iron electromagnet would cause the iron core to become

magnetized and therefore reluctant to release iron scraps when the current was turned off.

With AC current, the scraps could be released more easily.

2. In some apartment and office buildings, a tenant can "buzz" visitors into the building using a switch inside his or her unit. Explain how coils and currents work together to make this possible.

The lock on the outside door is most likely an electromagnetic lock. As long as current flows

through the circuit, the lock is held in place. The switch inside a unit allows an electric current

to flow and open the switch controlling the magnetic field holding the lock closed. The lock

will be open as long as the switch allows current to flow.

Date _____ Period _____ Name _____

24-1 Pocket Lab

Monopoles?

Place a disk magnet flat on the center of your paper. Place another disk magnet flat at the top of your paper and slowly slide it toward the center magnet.

Observing and Inferring

Does the first magnet attract or repel the second magnet? Rotate one of the magnets and note the effect on the other. Does each magnet have only one pole?

Depending upon the orientation of the two disks, they either attract or repel each other. Simply

rotating one of the magnets while it lies flat on the paper does not affect the other magnet. Each

magnet has two poles, which are oriented vertically.

24-2

Pocket Lab

Funny Balls

Place a disk magnet flat on your paper. Roll a 3-mm steel ball at the magnet. Place a second steel ball on the paper, touching the magnet and the first steel ball.

Hypothesizing

What happens? Why? Make a sketch to help explain your hypothesis. Devise a procedure to test your hypothesis.

The balls repel each other because both balls become magnetized with their axes pointing toward or away from the center of the bottom of the magnet. A small compass can be used to show that each ball really has a north and south pole.

_____

_____

_____

_____

_____

_____

24-3

Pocket Lab

3-D Magnetic Fields

Most illustrations are able to show the shape of the magnetic field around a magnet only two-dimensionally. Try this activity to see the shape of a magnetic field in 3-D. Tie a string to the middle of a nail so that the nail will hang horizontally. Put a small piece of tape around the string where it wraps around the nail so that the string will not slip. Insert the nail into a coil and apply a voltage to the coil. This will magnetize the nail. Turn off the power to the coil and remove the nail. Now hold the string to suspend the nail and slowly move it close to a permanent magnet. Try this for magnets of various shapes.

Analyze

What evidence do you have that the nail became magnetized? Using your results, make a 3-D drawing that shows the magnetic field around the nail.

The magnetic effect (field) extends in all directions from both poles and is therefore three-dimensional.

_____

_____

_____

_____

25 Design Your Own Physics Lab

Swinging Coils

Problem

Electricity that you use in your everyday life comes from the wall socket or from chemical batteries. Modern theory suggests that current can be caused by the interactions of wires and magnets. Exactly how do coils and magnets interact?

Hypothesis

Form a testable hypothesis that relates to the interaction of magnets and coils. Be sure to include some symmetry tests in your hypothesis. Try to design a system of coils and magnets so that you can use one pair as a generator and one pair as a motor.

Hypotheses should include the details of how the coils and magnets are to be arranged and moved. Hypotheses should also include some symmetry tests (e.g, pushing vs. pulling, North vs. South, etc.).

Plan the Experiment

1. Devise a means to test stationary effects: those that occur when the magnet and coils are not moving.

2. Consider how to test moving effects: those that occur when the magnet moves in various directions in relation to the coil.

3. Include different combinations of connecting, or not connecting, the ends of the wires.

4. Consider polarity, magnetic strength, and any other variables that might influence the interaction of the coils and magnet.

5. **Check the Plan** Make sure that your teacher has approved your final plan before you proceed with your experiment.

6. When you have completed the lab, dispose of or recycle appropriate materials. Put away materials that can be reused.

Analyze and Conclude

1. **Organizing Results** Construct a list of tests that you performed and their results.
   Tests will vary.

Possible Materials

coils of enameled wire
identical sets of magnets
masking tape
supports and bars

---

25 Physics Lab

2. **Analyzing Data** Summarize the effects of the stationary magnet and the moving magnet. Explain how connecting the wires influenced your results.
   The stationary magnet has no effect (copper is nonmagnetic) and the moving magnet still has no effect as long as the wires are disconnected. When a closed loop is formed, effects are seen: the coil swings in the opposite direction from the motion of the magnet.

3. **Relating Concepts** Describe and explain the effects of changing polarity, direction, number of coils, and any other variables you used.
   Reversing the direction of magnet motion reverses the direction of coil swing. When a second magnet is inside the second coil, then both coils swing. When the pole of the second magnet is reversed, the coil will swing in the opposite direction.

4. **Checking Your Hypothesis** Did the experiment yield expected results? Did you determine any new interactions?
   Answers will vary.

Apply

1. The current that you generated in this activity was quite small. List several factors that you could change to generate more current. (Hint: Think of a commercial generator.)
   Commercial generators have stronger magnets, the relative motion is much faster, and the number of coils is much greater. Each factor is important in determining the electrical energy.

25-1

Pocket Lab

Making Currents 🎵

Hook the ends of a 1-m length of wire to the binding posts of a galvanometer (or microammeter). Make several overlapping loops in the wire. Watch the readings on the wire as you move a pair of neodymium magnets (or a strong horseshoe magnet) near the loops. Record your observations.

Analyze and Conclude

What can you do to increase the current? Replace the 1-m length of wire with a preformed coil and see how much current you can produce. Describe your results.

The current is increased when the relative speed is greater, when the number of loops is

increased, and when the distance is smaller. The current is much greater when the coil is used.

_____

_____

_____

_____

_____

_____

_____

25-2

Pocket Lab

Motor and Generator 🎵

Make a series circuit with a Genecon (or efficient DC motor), a miniature lamp, and an ammeter. Rotate the handle (or motor shaft) to try to light the lamp.

Analyze and Conclude

Describe your results. Predict what might happen if you connect your Genecon to the Genecon from another lab group and crank yours. Try it. Describe what happens. Can more than two be connected? **When the Genecons are connected, one acts as a generator and the other acts as a motor.**

_____

_____

_____

_____

_____

_____

_____

_____

_____

_____

_____

25-3

Pocket Lab

Slow Motor

Make a series circuit with a miniature DC motor, an ammeter, and a DC power supply. Hook up a voltmeter in parallel across the motor. Adjust the setting on the power supply so that the motor is running at medium speed. Make a data table to show the readings on the ammeter and voltmeter.

Analyze and Conclude

Predict what will happen to the readings on the circuit when you hold the shaft and keep it from turning. Try it. Explain the results.

When the shaft of the motor is held, the back-*EMF* is reduced and the current increases.

25-4

Pocket Lab

Slow Magnet

Lay a 1-m length of copper tube on the lab table. Try to pull the copper with a pair of neodymium magnets. Can you feel any force on the copper? Hold the tube by one end so that it hangs straight down. Drop a small steel marble through the tube. Use a stopwatch to measure the time needed for first the marble and then for the pair of magnets to fall through the tube. Catch the magnets in your hand. If they hit the table or floor, they will break.

Analyze and Conclude

Devise a hypothesis that would explain the strange behavior of the falling magnets and suggest a method of testing your hypothesis.

The moving magnets induce a current in the copper. The current in the copper creates a magnetic field that acts opposite to the field of the magnets. Students can test this hypothesis by dropping magnets through a coil hooked to an ammeter.

26 ∿∿ Physics Lab

Simulating a Mass Spectrometer

Problem

How can you simulate the working parts of a mass spectrometer?

Materials

🐚 🧲🧲

2 balls of clay
grooved ruler
6-mm steel ball
glass marble
graph paper
masking tape
2 permanent magnets
cafeteria tray or glass wave
  tank

Procedure

1. Build the apparatus as shown in the diagram on page 612 of your textbook. Place a ball of clay under one side of the wave tank so that the tank is slightly sloped.

2. Make a test trial, allowing the steel ball to roll down the track. The ball should follow a curved path similar to the one shown in the diagram when it is started halfway up the ruler.

3. Starting from the same spot on the ruler, roll the steel ball down the track three times. Mark the positions where the ball crosses the far side of the graph paper.

4. Place the permanent magnets on the paper so they pull the ball slightly toward the high end of the slope. Adjust the magnets so that the ball follows a straight path across the graph paper, as shown in the diagram.

5. Releasing the ball from the same spot on the ruler, repeat step 3.

6. When you have completed the lab, dispose of or recycle appropriate materials. Put away materials that can be reused.

Data and Observations

1. Describe the path of the ball in step 3.
   The ball follows a parabolic curve. It accelerates downward.

2. Describe the path of the ball in step 5.
   The ball follows a straight line.

---

26 Physics Lab

Analyze and Conclude

1. **Thinking Critically** In this model, you used gravity to simulate the electric field of a mass spectrometer. How could the electric field in this model be varied?
   Increasing the slope of the wave tank would be similar to increasing the electric field.

2. **Analyzing Data** What happens to the path as the magnet is brought closer to the path of the ball? Why?
   The magnetic force increases as the magnet is brought closer to the ball. If the ball gets too close to the magnet, the ball will move upward.

3. **Thinking Critically** If you release the ball from a higher location, the ball will leave the ruler with more speed. In this case, the path will curve less, even though the force on the ball is the same. Why?
   A faster moving ball curves less because the force acts for less time.

Apply

1. Predict what would happen to a 6-mm ball that had the same mass, but less or no iron content. Explain your prediction. Test it.
   A ball with less iron content would not be affected as much by the magnets. A glass marble would not be affected by the magnets.

26-1

Pocket Lab

Rolling Along

Place a small ball of clay under one end of a grooved ruler to make a ramp. Roll a 6-mm-diameter steel ball down the ramp and along the tabletop. Place a strong magnet near the path of the ball so that the ball will curve, but not hit the magnet. Predict what will happen to the path when the ball is started higher or lower on the ramp. Try it.

Analyze and Conclude

Is this consistent for a charged particle moving through a magnetic field?

Yes, but in the case of the charged particle in a magnetic field, the particle curves less because

$r = mv/Bq$, **not because the field acts on it for less time.**

_____

_____

_____

_____

26-2

Pocket Lab

Catching the Wave

When you listen to your radio, you are hearing the information that is carried by electromagnetic waves. Many electronic and electrical devices produce low-frequency electromagnetic waves. Use a telephone pickup coil along with an amplifier to try to pick up signals from such devices as a television, computer, light, burning candle, coffee maker, or vacuum cleaner.

Analyzing Data

Describe and interpret your results.

Most appliances produce a humming sound at 60 Hz. Television sets produce a great deal of

electromagnetic waves. Computers and electronic balances also produce many electromagnetic

waves and will create a high-pitched whine. All the sounds are due to induced currents in the

pickup coil.

_____

_____

_____

_____

_____

_____

_____

26-3 Pocket Lab

More Radio Stuff

Radio stations broadcast with tremendous power from tall towers. Would it be possible to make your own radio transmitter and receiver? Try this activity to find out. Pop your favorite tape into a tape player, or tune your portable radio to a strong local AM station. Next, put a miniplug into the earphone jack, and attach the two leads to the ends of an air core solenoid. Put a second miniplug into a mini-amp speaker, and attach the leads to the ends of a second air core solenoid. Turn the power on for the miniamp speaker, and listen for the sound.

Make a Hypothesis

Make a hypothesis explaining why this lab works. Try changing the distance between the solenoids. Explain your results.

Students will find that the radio output produces a changing current in the solenoid, which causes a changing magnetic field around the solenoid. The changing magnetic field extends outward from the solenoid and moves through the second solenoid. This produces a changing current in the second solenoid, which is then converted into a sound signal by the mini-amp speaker. (The first solenoid acts as a transmitter, and the second acts as a receiver.) The signal gets weaker as the distance between the solenoids is increased.

_____

_____

_____

_____

_____

_____

---

27 Physics Lab

Red Hot or Not?

Problem

How well do steel balls simulate the photoelectric effect?

Procedure

1. Shape the grooved channel as shown in the diagram in your text-book on page 634. Mark a point on the channel, 4 cm above the table, with R for red.

2. Mark a point on the channel, 14 cm above the table, with V for violet. Place marks for blue, green, yellow, and orange uniformly between R and V.

3. Place two steel balls at the lowest point on the channel. These steel balls represent valence electrons in the atom.

4. Place a steel ball on the channel at the red mark. This represents a photon of red light, which has the lowest energy of the six colors of light being modeled.

5. Release the photon and see if the electrons are removed from the atom; that is, see if either steel ball escapes from the channel.

6. Remove the steel ball that represents the photon from the lower part of the channel.

7. Repeat steps 4–6 for each color's mark on the channel. **Note:** Always start with two electrons at the low point in the channel. Record your observations.

8. When you have completed the lab, dispose of or recycle appropriate materials. Put away materials that can be reused.

Materials

- 2-cm steel balls
- grooved channel (U-channel or shelf bracket)
- red, orange, yellow, green, blue, and violet marking pens or colored stickers

Data and Observations

1. Identify the photons by the color mark from which they were released. Which color of photons was able to remove the electrons? **Colors that have little energy per photon (red and yellow) will not remove an electron. Colors that have more energy per photon will push an electron from the atom.**

_____

_____

2. Did one photon ever remove more than one electron? If so, what was its color? **A single photon did not remove more than one electron.**

_____

27-1 Pocket Lab

Glows in the Dark

Close the shades and turn off the lights in the room. Shine a flashlight at a beaker that contains fluorescein. Now place a red filter over the flashlight so that only red light hits the beaker. Describe the results. Repeat the experiment using a green filter. Explain the results. Would you expect the fluorescein to glow when a blue filter is used? Explain your prediction. Try it.

Analyze and Conclude

Write a brief explanation of your observations.

Light with wavelength shorter than green light has energy sufficient to cause the fluorescein to glow.

---

27 Physics Lab

3. Summarize your observations in terms of the energies of the photons.

Students should clearly state the following ideas: (a) Photons that start above a certain energy level will always remove a valence electron. (b) A single photon can remove only a single valence electron.

Analyze and Conclude

1. **Making Predictions** Predict what would happen if two red photons could hit the electrons at the same time.

Most students will predict that two red photons should have sufficient energy to remove one electron. This is incorrect.

2. **Testing Predictions** Start two steel balls (photons) at the red mark on the channel and see what happens. Describe the results.

Rolling two photons down the channel causes two electrons to move, but not enough to remove both of them from the atom.

3. **Making Inferences** Some materials hold their valence electrons tighter than others. How could the model be modified to show this?

The short end of the channel should be made longer or steeper to model a material that has a tighter hold on its valence electrons.

Apply

1. Photographers often have red lights in their darkrooms. Explain why they use red light but not blue light.

Photographers use red light because red has low energy per photon and will not cause a chemical change in exposed film. Blue light has more energy per photon and would affect the film.

27-2

Pocket Lab

See the Light

Close the shades and turn off all the lights in the room. Look at a 150-W lamp as you use a dimmer switch to slowly increase and decrease the voltage across the lamp. Describe what you observe. What would you expect to see if you repeated the experiment while looking through a diffraction grating? Why? Try it. Describe your results.

Analyze and Conclude

Describe your observations.

The frequency and the energy of the light are proportional to the voltage. Using a diffraction

grating, all colors are visible at high voltages.

_____

_____

_____

_____

_____

_____

_____

_____

_____

_____

28

Physics Lab

Shots in the Dark

Problem

Given that the atom is mostly empty space, how easy is it to it to hit a nucleus and cause atomic scattering?

Procedure

1. Construct the model according to the diagram in your textbook on page 656.

2. Each student will be blindfolded, led to a position 3 m directly in front of the target area, and allowed to toss ten rubber stoppers (one at a time) into the target area. If a rubber stopper does not strike within the target area, the shooter should be told "too high," "too low," and so on and be given an extra rubber stopper.

3. Students will be able to hear the nuclear "hit" when the rubber stopper hits the target area. Only one hit will be counted on a single target.

4. When you have completed the lab, dispose of or recycle appropriate materials. Put away materials that can be reused.

Materials

- 3 dozen rubber stoppers
- bedsheet (or blanket)
- blindfold (or darkened goggles)
- six 9-inch aluminum pie pans
- four 1.5-meter 1×2 wood pieces
- fishing line

Data and Observations

Table 1		
Student's Name	Number of Shots	Number of Hits

28 Physics Lab

Name _____

Analyze and Conclude

There are six circular targets within the target area. The ratio of hits to shots is represented by the following:

$$\frac{hits}{shots} = \frac{total\ target\ area}{total\ model\ area} = \frac{6\pi r^2}{width \times height}$$

1. **Analyzing Data** Use the class totals for shots and hits to calculate the total area for the six targets. Estimate the area for each target. Then calculate the radius for each target.

Students should use the equation: hits/shots = $6\pi r^2$/(height × width).

2. **Relating Concepts** The uncertainty for this experiment decreases with more shots. The percentage uncertainty is represented by the following:

$$\%\ uncertainty = \frac{(shots)^{1/2}}{shots} \times 100$$

Find the uncertainty for your class.

For 25 students with ten shots each, % uncertainty = $(250)^{1/2}$/250 × 100 = 6.3%.

Apply

1. A recent phone poll sampled 800 people. Estimate the uncertainty in the poll.

The percent uncertainty in the telephone poll is $(800)^{1/2}$/800 × 100 = 3.5%.

Physics Lab and Pocket Lab Worksheets

Physics: Principles and Problems

Date _____ Period _____ Name _____

28-1

Pocket Lab

Nuclear Bouncing 🔊

Place a 9-inch aluminum pie pan on a table. Gently press four glass marbles (protons) into the pie pan so that they sit in small indentations near the center of the pan. Roll a 12-mm steel ball (alpha particle) down a grooved ruler to see if you can hit the marbles. Then remove the marbles and put the steel balls into the indentations (each steel ball represents a nucleus) in the pie pan and roll a marble (alpha particle) down the grooved ruler.

Analyze and Conclude

When you roll the steel ball at the marbles, does it change its path? Does the steel ball ever bounce back? When you switch the balls and marbles, how are the results different? Why are the results different? Hypothesize what will happen when an alpha particle hits a proton.

The glass marble changes direction by large angles when it hits the more massive steel balls.

Physics: Principles and Problems

Physics Lab and Pocket Lab Worksheets **153**

70T *Teacher Guide and Answers*

Physics: Principles and Problems

28-2

Pocket Lab

Bright Lines

Turn on a gas-discharge tube power supply attached to a gas tube so that the tube glows. **CAUTION: Do not touch any exposed metal when the power supply is turned on.** *Dangerous high voltages are present. Always turn off the power supply before changing gas tubes.* Turn off the room lights. Describe the color. Now look through a diffraction grating at the tube.

Analyze and Conclude

Make a sketch of the results. Repeat this activity with a different gas tube. Explain the differences.

The colors and spacing of the lines depend on the electron energy levels within the gas.

_____

_____

_____

_____

_____

_____

28-3

Pocket Lab

Laser Diffraction

CAUTION: *Avoid staring directly into the laser beam or at bright reflections.* A diffraction grating separates light from discharge tubes into individual wavelengths. Predict what will happen when you shine a laser light through a diffraction grating. Shine the laser at a sheet of white paper about 1 foot away. Then place the diffraction grating next to the laser to see what happens.

Analyze and Conclude

Describe and explain your results. Predict how your results would be similar and different with a green laser light.

A green laser would produce green spots, but in different positions because the green laser would

have a different wavelength.

_____

_____

_____

_____

_____

_____

_____

29 〰 Physics Lab

The Stoplight

Problem

How can you design a circuit so that changing the direction of the current changes the LED that lights up?

Materials

0- to 12-V variable power supply
red LED
green LED
bicolored LED
wires
470-Ω resistor
voltmeter

Procedure

1. Connect a series circuit with the power supply, the resistor, and the red and green LEDs to light them both. Do not bypass or omit the resistor with an LED. Always have the resistor between an LED and one side of the power supply.

2. Reverse the direction of the current in the circuit and note the result. Measure the voltage across an LED.

3. Design a circuit so that changing the direction of the current will change the color that lights up.

4. Test your circuit.

5. When you have completed the lab, dispose of or recycle appropriate materials. Put away materials that can be reused.

Data and Observations

1. What voltage was needed to light the LEDs?
The LEDs will begin to glow around 1.8 V and be bright at 2.2 V (measured across the LED).

2. Describe what happened when the current was reversed.
Reversing the current causes both LEDs to go out.

Analyze and Conclude

1. **Diagramming a Circuit** Make a drawing to show your stoplight circuit (red on, green off; then green on, red off).
The stoplight circuit will have the LEDs in parallel branches and reversed in polarity.

---

29 Physics Lab

2. **Explaining Results** Why does your stoplight circuit work?
By reversing the polarity of the LEDs, only one color can be *on* at a time. Reversing the leads at the power supply will change the color of the stoplight.

3. **Analyzing Results** Is your circuit a series or parallel circuit?
It is a series circuit. However, to light both the red and green LEDs at the same time, the LEDs must be connected in parallel.

4. **Making Predictions** What change would you observe if you replaced the resistor with a 330-Ω resistor?
The 330-Ω resistor allows more current to flow through the circuit, causing the LEDs to glow more brightly.

5. **Forming a Hypothesis** If the voltage across the LED was increased, what would happen to the current?
Because $V = IR$, students will likely indicate that current increases as voltage increases.

6. **Thinking Critically** What must be true for the graph or current versus voltage to be a straight line?
The graph will be a straight line only if the resistance remains constant. (It does not.)

Apply

1. Design and conduct experiments to discover what type of LED the bicolored LED is. Remember to leave the resistor connected to the power supply.
The bicolor LED will be green when the current flows in one direction and red when the current flows in the opposite direction.

2. How does an LED differ from a 60-W lightbulb?
A lightbulb emits a broad range of the electromagnetic spectrum, whereas an LED emits a single wavelength only. In addition, current can pass either way across a lightbulb filament but only in one direction through an LED.

29-1

Pocket Lab

All Aboard! 🔌 ⚡

Metals become better conductors when they are cooled. Semiconductors become better conductors when they are heated. Does a thermistor act like a metal or a semiconductor?

Make a series circuit with a low-voltage DC power supply, a thermistor, and an ammeter (0–100 mA scale). Slowly turn up the power supply until the needle is in the middle of the scale (50 mA). The voltage will be about 0.6 V. Watch what happens to the current when you hold the thermistor between your fingers. Describe the results.

_____
_____
_____

Comparing and Contrasting

List several possible advantages of thermistors over standard thermometers.

Thermistors are smaller, cheaper, more durable, and can be directly connected into electronic circuits.

_____
_____
_____
_____

29-2

Pocket Lab

Red Light ⚡ 🔌

Make a series circuit with a power supply, a 470-Ω resistor, and a red LED. Connect the short lead of the LED to the negative side of the power supply. Attach the other lead to the resistor. Hook the remaining resistor lead to the positive side of the power supply. Slowly increase the voltage until the LED glows. Note the voltage setting on the power supply.

Hypothesize

What will happen if you reverse the direction of current? Why? Try it and explain what happens.

The LED will allow current to flow in only one direction.

_____
_____
_____
_____
_____
_____
_____
_____

30 ⋙ Physics Lab

Heads Up

Problem

How does the activity of radioactive materials decrease over time? Devise a model of the radioactive decay system.

Materials

20 pennies
graph paper

Procedure

1. Set up a data table as shown, or use a spreadsheet. Turn the pennies so that they are all heads. In this simulation, a heads indicates that the nucleus has not decayed.

2. Flip each coin separately and put the heads and tails into separate piles.

3. Record the number of heads on your data sheet or spreadsheet. Remove the pennies that came up tails.

4. Flip all remaining coins and separate the heads and tails. Count the number of heads and record the value.

5. Repeat steps 2–4 one more time.

6. Share your data with four other students and copy their data onto your data sheet or spreadsheet.

Data and Observations

Table 1

	You	Other Students				Total
Begin	20	20	20	20	20	100
Trial 1						
Trial 2						
Trial 3						

---

30 Physics Lab

Analyze and Conclude

1. **Comparing Data** Did each person have the same number of heads after each trial? **Student answers will vary.**

2. **Analyzing Data** Is the number of heads close to what you expected? **Most students will get about half heads each trial, but a few may get large discrepancies.**

3. **Graphing Results** Total the number of heads remaining for each trial. Make a graph of the number of heads (vertical) verses the trial (horizontal). If possible, use a graphing calculator or a computer plotting program. **Graphs should be similar to the theoretical graph shown in the textbook on page 700.**

4. **Interpreting Graphs** Evaluate and compare your results to the theoretical graph shown in the lab on page 700 of your textbook. Propose explanations for any differences you notice. **The actual data will show the same type of curve as the theoretical graph. Low sample size contributes to a difference between actual and theoretical.**

5. **Understanding Procedures** Explain the rationale for collecting the results from other students and using the sum of all the results for graphing and analysis. **Combining student data will likely smooth out individual variations. Increasing the sample size also improves results.**

Apply

1. Radioactive materials are often used in medicine for diagnostic purposes. Are these radioisotopes likely to have a short or a long half-life? Explain. **The radioisotope would have a short half-life. This would mean it would be in a person's system only a short time, thereby reducing the harmful effects of the radiation.**

2. Laws mandate that hospitals keep radioactive materials for 10 half-lives before disposing of them. Calculate the fraction of the original activity left at the end of 10 half-lives. **After 10 half-lives, the activity will be 0.098% of the original rate.**

30-1

Pocket Lab

Background Radiation

Place a Geiger counter on the lab table far away from any sources of radiation. Turn the counter on and record the number of counts for a three-minute interval. Tape a piece of paper around the tube to cover the window and repeat the measurements.

Analyze and Conclude

Did the count go down? What type of radiation could the counter be receiving? Explain.

A random count has an uncertainty equal to the square root of the number of counts recorded.

Thus, two counts are statistically different only if they differ by several multiples of the uncertainty

in each count. You may have to count for an hour or more to determine if your have a difference.

Background radiation consists primarily of gamma rays.

_____

_____

_____

_____

_____

_____

30-2

Pocket Lab

Follow the Tracks

CAUTION: *Avoid extended contact with a radioactive source. Handle with extreme caution.* Prepare a cloud chamber by soaking the cloth ring in alcohol. Place the radioactive needle into the side of the cloud chamber and then place the chamber on a block of dry ice. After the chamber cools down, you should be able to observe the tracks of the radiation.

Analyze and Conclude

Predict what might happen when you place a small neodymium magnet in the bottom of the center of the chamber. Try it. Describe the results.

Because the alpha particles are charged, they will follow a curved path in the presence of

a magnetic field. Students should form a lasting impression of this activity.

_____

_____

_____

_____

_____

_____

_____

_____

31))))) Physics Lab

Solar Power

Problem

How can you measure the local power output from the nearest continuous running fusion reactor, the sun?

Procedure

1. With no load attached, measure the voltage output of a solar cell when the cell is outdoors and directly facing the sun.
2. Measure the current from the solar cell when the cell is outdoors and directly facing the sun.
3. Measure the length and width of the solar cell and determine its surface area.
4. Remeasure the voltage and current when the sunlight passes through a window.

Data and Observations

Table 1

Voltage Indoor	Voltage Outdoor	Current Indoor	Current Outdoor

Materials

solar cell
voltmeter
ammeter
electrical leads
ruler

---

31 Physics Lab

Analyze and Conclude

1. **Calculating Results** Calculate the power, IV, for the solar cell outdoors and indoors. What percentage of power did the window stop?

    The typical power for a 4-cm × 10-cm solar cell is 0.45 W. Student answers will vary depending on the time of day. If the sun strikes the window directly, nearly all the power will pass through. If the sun hits the window at a very oblique angle, the window may stop up to 80% of the power.

2. **Calculating Results** Calculate the amount of power that could be produced by a cell that has an area of 1.0 square meter.

    The typical cell could produce about 110 W for each square meter.

3. **Calculating Efficiency** The sun supplies about 1000 W of power per square meter to Earth. Calculate the efficiency of your solar cell.

    The efficiency of most readily available solar cells should be in the range of 10% to 15%.

Apply

1. You are planning to install 15 square meters of solar cells on your roof. How much power will you expect them to produce?

    Fifteen square meters of solar cells could collect 15 000 W of sunlight. At 15% efficiency, the electrical output would be 2.3 kW.

2. Solar panels are used to power satellites in orbit. These panels are generally more efficient than those used on Earth. Why, then, do the satellites still carry batteries?

    The solar cells cannot produce electricity when a satellite is in Earth's shadow. Further, batteries offer a backup power source should the solar panels become damaged or disabled.

31-1

Pocket Lab

Binding Energy

Particles within the nucleus are strongly bonded. Place two disk magnets together to represent a proton and neutron within a nucleus. Slowly pull them apart. Feel how the force changes with separation.

Analyze and Conclude

Describe how this analogy could be extended for a nucleus that contains several protons and neutrons.
The strong force holding this nucleus together acts only when the particles are touching.

31-2

Pocket Lab

Power Plant

Call your local electric company and ask the following questions.

1. Where is the nearest nuclear power plant?

2. What fraction (or percentage) of electricity is supplied by nuclear power in your area?

Analyze and Conclude

How much electrical energy in your neighborhood is provided by nuclear power and how much is provided by other sources?
Students should find that nuclear power provides some of the electricity used in their area.

The actual amounts will vary.

Notes